EXPAND THE CIRCLE

EXPAND THE CIRCLE

ENLIGHTENED LEADERSHIP FOR OUR NEW WORLD OF WORK

MATT POEPSEL

NEW DEGREE PRESS

COPYRIGHT © 2023 MATT POEPSEL

All rights reserved.

EXPAND THE CIRCLE

Enlightened Leadership for Our New World of Work

ISBN   979-8-88926-651-8 *Paperback*
          979-8-88926-650-1 *Ebook*
          979-8-88926-652-5 *Hardcover*

For my teachers:

Past. Present. Future. Timeless.

CONTENTS

———

INTRODUCTION

———

Arianna Huffington was working from her home office one April morning. Rather than sitting behind her desk, however, she found herself lying next to it in a pool of blood. A lengthy string of eighteen-hour workdays had left her completely depleted. She collapsed from exhaustion while standing, and she hit her head on the corner of the desk on her way down. While her broken cheekbone healed, she reflected on her life. She concluded that there's more to life than money and power even though she had plenty of both. "I knew something had to change. I could not go on that way," she later wrote. "This was a classic wake-up call" (Huffington 2014, 2).

In early 2020, a very different wake-up call wrenched millions of workers from their collective slumber.

The COVID-19 pandemic accelerated two developments that had been steadily percolating for more than a decade. The first impacted the work. While a mere 6 percent of white-collar employees worked remotely prior to the pandemic, that number skyrocketed to 65 percent at its height (Goldberg 2022). Many businesses put their digital transformation efforts into hyperdrive, and many more had to overhaul their business models to adapt to new consumer trends brought on by this seismic shift.

The second upheaval hit even closer to home. Many workers reevaluated and reprioritized their deepest held personal values. They experienced a heightened sense of awareness of what mattered most to them as well as an increased sense of self-worth (Wiles 2022). Societal challenges such as social unrest, a polarized political climate, and senseless violence exacerbated workers' uneasiness about the world and their place in it. As affected employees prepared for their next day's work, they silently asked themselves, "Why am I doing this?"

Like a bad breakup, many workers lamented, "It's not me, work. It's *you*."

In early 2022, more than four million US employees quit their jobs *each month* (Maurer 2022). Average employee engagement dropped for the first time in a decade (Harter 2002). Workers continued experiencing tremendous pressure and anxiety borne of factors from inside and outside the workplace. Nearly a third of workers reported that their mental health declined over the past year (Lyra Health, n.d.). This led to an observation that "employees' mental health is at an all-time low." Even when a worker took a new job, there was a chance they might not stick. In a survey, 80 percent of millennial and Generation Z candidates said they would leave a new job in fewer than six months if it didn't meet their expectations (Tomb 2022).

In response, employers went to great lengths to attract and retain high performing workers. They sweetened their compensation, benefits packages, and perks. In economic terms, the average employee's quality of life has never been higher. Employers feel workers *should* be happy, but their employees continue to walk away from their jobs or struggle in silence. So, where's the disconnect?

A McKinsey study revealed that workers and employers view workers' unfulfilled needs very differently (Smet et al. 2021). Employees rated several work-related needs as being more important to them than their employers did: being valued by their organizations, being valued by their managers, having a sense of belonging, and having caring and trusting teammates.

Psychologist Abraham Maslow (1943) introduced his well-known hierarchy of needs to demystify human motivations. He asserted that we experience ascending layers of needs ranging from basic needs such as food, water, and shelter at the bottom to safety, relationship, esteem, and other higher-order needs at the peak of our experience.

Many workers today find they can adequately meet their basic and even mid-level needs through virtually *any* employer. Beyond that, they continue to experience what I refer to as the three "Killer Bs": Being, Belonging, and something Bigger than myself. I call these *Killer* Bs because when we fail to satisfy them, it kills our productivity, engagement, performance, and intent to stay. These needs have always been a part of our human condition, it's just that now we're seeing and experiencing them in an entirely new way.

This view of the work and the worker is incomplete, however. It implies that an inherent disconnect exists in the modern workplace. What's missing is something that can help workers meet their existential needs while performing meaningful and necessary work in organizations. Fortunately, there *is* something that can be that bridge; leadership can make the critical connection.

Leadership has always evolved alongside the work and the worker. It progressed from authoritarian leadership through transformational leadership and more recently servant leadership, to name but a few approaches. The challenge is that contemporary leadership theories weren't designed to accommodate today's work nor today's worker.

It's time for us to enter the next era of leadership.

I've studied effective leadership for more than thirty years. I began my adult working life in the United States Marine Corps where my first day on the job began well before the sun came up. My loving drill instructors immediately provided me with two things most civilian onboarding programs lack: a clean-shaven head and a book of leadership principles.

When I transitioned to the corporate world six years later, I wanted to continue my leadership education. I was told that I was on my own; no formal leadership development program was available for me or my coworkers. A trunk full of audiobooks and a lengthy commute kept me in learning mode.

After several years of applying leadership lessons and earning promotions, I studied leadership and coaching at the highest level, earning a PhD in psychology. I completed my Certificate of Management Excellence from Harvard Business School where I participated in an intensive course on Authentic Leadership Development. Along the way, I joined The Predictive Index, a workforce assessment and advisory company where I studied leadership traits, successes, and failures across thousands of companies.

Then I hit my head.

Not literally like Huffington, but I experienced a profound wake-up call all the same. Like so many millions of people, the aftershock of the pandemic pressed me into survival mode. This showed up most clearly in my professional life. After months of heads-down work leading our software product teams, I was burned out. My effectiveness had waned, I took no joy from my day-to-day work, and my to-do list looked about as enticing as a head wound. Worst of all, I felt I had hit the limit of my leadership ability. I wasn't showing up for my people the way I wanted, and they deserved far better.

I came face-to-face with my Killer Bs:

Being: "Who am I really?"

Belonging: "Where do I fit in?"

Bigger than myself: "How does what I'm doing make a difference in the world?"

I considered walking away from my company, from the work I had done for more than twenty years, and from my professional identity. I wanted to be anywhere but here.

While I was pondering my place in the universe, my father received a dreaded call from his oncologist. In the months that followed, my father would undergo a major surgery and a lengthy recovery. His diagnosis jostled my perspective and my priorities.

I went to my bookshelf and withdrew a book I hadn't cracked in more than fifteen years. *The Tibetan Book of Living and Dying* made two claims that resonated deeply with me in that moment. The first is that each of us will die someday. In fairness, I suspected as much. The second is that when that moment inevitably comes, to die well, we must first learn how to live well (Rinpoche, Gaffney, and Harvey 2002).

"Well, shit," I thought to myself. "I am absolutely *not* living well."

I resumed my long-abandoned practice of meditation, and I studied ancient texts. I soon discovered a meditation practice known as *tonglen*. It involves "taking in" the suffering experienced by others and "sending out" compassion and peace. The meditator first does this for themselves, then for their inner circle of loved ones, then with strangers, and ultimately out into an expanded circle encompassing all beings throughout the universe.

As a novice meditator, I spend much of my time on the cushion thinking about work. In my defense, Buddha didn't have unread Slack messages and a Zoom call at 9:00 a.m. sharp. However, my deep study of Buddhist philosophy and Western leadership collided on the cushion to produce a delightful discovery:

Enlightened leadership can liberate us as leaders and transform those around us.

I was awakened from my slumber. I fashioned my insight into a new leadership approach, and I began incorporating it into my daily practice. I taught it to other leaders. The results have been profound.

My approach has several important characteristics; it's simple to understand and remember, it's grounded in contemporary social science, it draws on the real-world business environment, and it evokes the type of compassion that our world desperately needs right now.

I call the approach "Expand the Circle." This book presents the elements of this approach and how you can apply them in your own leadership across five progressive layers:
- Lead Yourself: I'll teach you how to practice self-mastery.
- Lead Others: you'll learn how to make critical connections with a direct report, peer, or manager.
- Lead Your Team: we'll discover how to unite a group in the pursuit of a collective goal.
- Lead Your Organization: you'll learn how to create and reinforce people-centric practices at scale.
- Lead the World: we'll go beyond the boundaries of an organization by extending our impact and positivity into the broader world system.

This book is designed to benefit leaders at every level of an organization, as you are in the best position to make a critical connection with an individual and satisfy the full range of their needs. Specific situations often spur leaders to seek development. These include individual contributors who wish to develop their leadership skills and aspiring leaders who seek to be promoted. Also included are those receiving first-time leadership appointments, leaders who've hit a plateau in their effectiveness and satisfaction, and leaders who've received a difficult performance rating. Wherever you are on your leadership journey, I'm glad you've come to this place.

I've also written this book for you executives and team leaders who wish to bring the gift of leadership to your managers and individual contributors, both as a means of investing in them and reaping the benefits of improved organizational performance. For you HR leaders who wish to equip your line of business leaders with an inspiring and actionable framework, you'll also find what you seek in this book.

Huffington gained clarity following her calamity, realizing "the timeless truth that life is shaped from the inside out—a truth that has been celebrated by spiritual teachers, poets, and philosophers throughout the ages, and has now been validated by modern science" (Huffington 2014, 260). We can shape our lives, the lives of those around us, and the entire world if we approach our work from the inside out. We can Expand the Circle.

Along the way we'll reunite with familiar management thinkers like Adam Grant, Amy Edmondson, and Simon Sinek. We'll meet new leadership luminaries like Hema Crockett,

Raj Sisodia, and Henry Schuck. Our adventures will take us deep beneath the sea and up into the endless blue sky. We'll draw lessons from the most unusual sources including walnut groves, high speed trains, and the quantum mechanics that both govern the universe and fuel its delusion.

When you Expand the Circle, you take your leadership to the next level. You produce better results for your organization. You meet the needs of those around you, and you help them reduce their suffering. Your mastery spills over and benefits the world that lies beyond your organization. You invite change, and you are forever changed.

Each time we Expand the Circle, we make a ripple in the ocean of work. Enough ripples turn into swells, and swells become great waves—waves that can wash away the fears, anxieties, and disconnects that plague our workplaces and the well-being of our workers.

Over the course of my career, I've attempted to unravel the mystery of leadership only to discover that the final clue was locked in a 2,500-year-old vault. What I found there has helped me light a new path, but only you can walk it.

I'm glad to be on this journey with you. Let's begin by taking a deeper look at how we got to this place and where we go from here.

THE NEW WORLD
OF WORK

———

*It is not the strongest of the species that survives, nor the most
intelligent; it is the one most adaptable to change.*

—*CHARLES DARWIN*

Grand Canyon National Park is larger than the state of Rhode
Island. The size of the canyon itself is equally staggering. It
measures as much as ten miles across and more than a mile
deep. Looking up from the base of the canyon is a surreal experience. You find yourself surrounded by smooth brown rock
on all sides with only a slit of blue sky above. From this unique
vantage point, you begin to understand why the Hopi tribe
consider the Grand Canyon to be a gateway to the afterlife.

Some of the rock in the canyon is more than 1.8 billion years
old. As you run your fingertips along a section of sedimen-
tary rock, you feel the protruding bumps of fossils that have
been entombed there for thousands of millennia. These aren't
the remnants of desert dwellers, however. They belong to

various marine species that swam or crawled in a vast body of water that once covered a significant portion of the current Southwestern United States (National Parks Service, n.d.).

In the natural world, oceans become deserts and land masses splinter into thousands of tiny islands. Earth's inhabitants adapt to their new surroundings accordingly. Our world is in a constant state of evolution.

Our world of work is no different.

We humans have been punching the proverbial clock since prehistoric times. Our work, economies, and societies have all evolved as we've pooled our intellect and resources. For all its complexity, the world of work can be broken down into three basic components:

To best understand the state of today's world of work, we need to examine where each of these components has been.

EVOLUTION OF THE WORK CONTEXT

Our work has undergone a constant progression from our most primal beginnings to the modern organization.

Hunter-Gatherer

Humans work to fulfill their basic needs for food, water, shelter, and clothing. In these prehistoric times, the term "rock and roll" would have referred to a pillow and our most significant invention to date. For the most part, everybody works in relative isolation.

Agrarian Age

Humans begin to plant crops, domesticate certain helpful animals, and settle down. The first societies form as do the large settlements that enable them to function. Examples include those in Mesopotamia, Egypt, the Indus Valley, and the Andes Mountains.

Industrial Age

Rudimentary factories spew out a tremendous volume of products, clothing, and food items. More sophisticated factories begin to produce steel, electronics, and automobiles. For all its technological advancements, factory work is plagued by inhospitable working conditions.

Post-Industrial Age

The services economy begins to displace heavy industry in many large urban areas. Jobs outside the factory setting include those in engineering, medicine, and banking. The nature of the work shifts from manual labor and assembly lines to human capital and specialized skills.

Knowledge/Connected Age
Creative and intellectual work takes place in accounting firms, Hollywood studios, and software development companies. The advent of the Internet spawns collaborative and networked forms of work including increasingly popular remote and hybrid work formats. *Social Media Influencer* somehow becomes a legit job.

Conscious Capitalism
A gradual shift toward Corporate Social Responsibility (CSR) reflects an increasing demand that organizations be thoughtful and transparent about the impact they have on the broader society. Environmental, Social, and Governance (ESG) provides a means of quantifying and benchmarking an organization's impact on important stakeholders beyond the organization's own interests.

While the byproduct of prehistoric work was aimed at satisfying an individual's or a small group's basic needs, modern enterprise is dramatically different. Organizations today have benefitted from multiple millennia of steadily increasing innovation, scale, and sophistication. The most progressive organizations now seek to serve a diverse range of stakeholders who are both directly and indirectly connected to those organizations' strategies and operations.

EVOLUTION OF WORKER NEEDS

Maslow's famous hierarchy of needs provides a bottom-to-top view into the range of motivating factors we each experience.

Physiological Needs

Physiological needs for adequate food, air, water, shelter, and clothing are the most basic needs a worker experiences and seeks to satisfy. Coffee somehow fails to make the list at this level but just barely.

Safety Needs

Once those basic order needs are satisfied, safety needs become important. A worker needs to feel secure in terms of their physical and psychological safety as well as the stability of their working environment.

Relationship Needs

A worker's relationships with family members, a romantic partner, coworkers, and friends are impacted by experiences at work. Affiliation, belonging, and camaraderie are important needs, but office birthday parties are still best avoided at all costs.

Esteem Needs

The worker experiences a desire to learn, pursue mastery, and achieve personal growth. They have a strong interest in professional and personal development as well as autonomy over discretionary investments of their time, energy, and attention.

Self-Actualization Needs

The worker seeks to become totally engrossed in their work, enter a satisfying "flow state," and reach the pinnacle of their perceived potential and contribution.

Self-Transcendence Needs

The worker feels a desire to escape their own self-interest entirely. They seek greater connection and service to something larger than themself. Self-transcendence extends their attention and effort out into the broader reaches of society and the world at large.

As the work context has steadily evolved over time, workers have generally found it easier to satisfy their lower-order needs. Earlier generations of workers toiled in return for survival or safety. By comparison, modern workers enjoy a much more comfortable standard of living. The average worker's needs, particularly for those living in developed economies, have graduated toward higher-order concerns.

EVOLUTION OF LEADERSHIP APPROACHES

Not to be outdone, leadership theories and styles have continually progressed toward a more humanistic worldview over time.

Authoritarian

The strength of the ruling class is used to subjugate workers to do the most manual and menial work. Slavery, serfdom, and militaristic organizations prioritize work output over worker welfare.

Transactional

Exchange theory focuses on tit-for-tat techniques. The employer provides minimal wages in exchange for the work to be done and nothing more. This leadership attitude and approach became common practice in industrialized work, and it remains all too popular in many crappy organizations today.

Transformational

Attention shifts to emphasizing the relationship between the leader and their followers. The nature of the relationship and the benefit both parties receive from it becomes the means to superior business results, individual performance, and achievement.

Servant

The leader places the needs of the follower above their own. A supportive coaching role is preferred to a directive leadership style, and the leader seeks to help the worker identify possibilities and remove barriers.

Authentic

The leader seeks to understand and connect with the joys and frustrations they've faced in their work and personal life. Their focus is on living with integrity and a sense of purpose as well as bringing the full depth of idealized potential into practice.

Early forms of leadership centered almost exclusively on worker output with a nearly complete disregard for worker welfare. Over time, new leadership approaches progressed to reflect an approach that balances the need for business results with the interests and well-being of those doing the work. The linkage is clear: an evolution in work and society leads to an evolution in the human condition. Leadership approaches, therefore, must continually follow suit.

THE NEW WORLD OF WORK

At present, our world of work is a world divided.

While the work and the needs of the worker have changed dramatically, many workplaces lag and are still focused on serving workers' middle-order needs. Therefore, although employers feel they are offering hefty benefits packages and unprecedented flexibility, employees are still looking for more.

Modern workers often find they can satisfy their most basic needs at just about any job, but they still feel pressing needs of the higher-order variety in the form of the Killer Bs. Experts have taken notice. One notable headline from management consulting firm McKinsey cautions executives, "Help your employees find purpose—or watch them leave" (Dhingra et al. 2021).

While leadership *has* evolved over time, it has failed to keep up with the latest progression of the work and the needs of the worker. When we compare these entangled evolutions side by side, we notice there's a gap:

Uh oh.

	WORK CONTEXT	WORKER NEEDS	LEADERSHIP APPROACH
Higher Order	Conscious Capitalism	Self-Transcendence	
	Knowledge/Connected	Self-Actualization	Authentic
	Post-Industrial	Esteem	Servant
	Industrial	Relationship	Transformational
	Agrarian	Safety	Transactional
Lower Order	Hunter Gatherer	Physiological	Authoritarian

When it comes to worker needs satisfaction, the elevator keeps going up and up. It's as if employees are in the penthouse suite while employers and leaders are stuck on the middle floors. Each is asking the other "Where are you?"

The gap between the two sides is as wide as a certain canyon situated in the Arizona desert.

Unmet worker needs have consequences in terms of business performance, employee experience, or both. One inevitable risk is turnover. A study by the consulting firm PwC (2022) revealed "money isn't enough to retain workers," and employees cited a lack of meaning as a major motivation to leave their current employers. In fact, job fulfillment and "the ability to be one's true self at work" rounded out the top three deciding factors for these prospective job jumpers. When focusing specifically on workers with one eye on the door, this group was less likely to feel "their team cares about them" or "their manager listens to them." The firm's survey from the prior year also aligned with the Killer Bs, noting, "75 percent of employees said they wanted to work for an organization that makes a positive contribution to society."

Another study on the future of work from Korn Ferry (2021) produced similar findings. The authors concluded, "Employees are now starting to ask human questions about the work they perform." Again, having one's basic needs met only raises the stakes, leading the worker to experience higher-order needs. The report's authors provided employers with the type of advice that would seem obvious to any first grader yet is often overlooked by the average first line manager. "Treat employees as human beings," the authors recommended. "Ensure people feel connected to the company purpose and vision and each other."

When workers' higher-order needs go unmet, other devastating side effects beyond turnover appear. Stress and burnout are on the rise. According to a global study by the payroll company ADP (2022), "COVID-19 triggered a reevaluation of what job security means to workers." As a result, many began to reprioritize their current levels of well-being and the quality of life they enjoy outside of work.

The disconnect is taking a toll. Two-thirds of workers surveyed claim to experience stress at work weekly, and 15 percent experience stress daily. The ill effects trickle down to the bottom line. Over half of those surveyed "believe their work is suffering because of poor mental health." Making matters worse, the damage isn't constrained to the workplace. A study by Mental Health America (n.d.) found that four in five employees reported that stress at work had affected relationships with their friends, families, and coworkers.

These trends make it clear: when workers' needs outstrip their ability to satisfy their cravings, suffering ensues and happiness at work is fleeting.

This isn't a new problem, of course. I became very empathetic to this predicament when I noticed more and more people around me at work who were frustrated or unfulfilled. Regardless of their job function, seniority, education, or amount of compensation, I saw people who were in pain.

This led me to pursue my PhD in psychology. I wanted to study leadership and coaching and learn how I might address the level of frustration and disconnect workers are experiencing. I wanted to connect them with the positive psychology of personal growth and achievement.

I didn't realize at the time that I'd soon complement my love of Western psychology journals and coaching techniques with Eastern philosophical texts and meditation practice.

THE DAWN OF ENLIGHTENED LEADERSHIP

In the Cambridge English Dictionary, the term *enlightened* is doubly defined as:

> a. open to new ideas and facts based on reason and science rather than following old, false beliefs; and
> b. knowing the truth about existence.

On that basis, I define *enlightened leadership* as:

> A leadership approach characterized by opening oneself to new beliefs and practices inspired by ancient wisdom and grounded in modern science.

We don't have to reach enlightenment in the Buddhist sense to become awakened to a better leadership approach. Simply learning enlightened leadership principles, aspiring to bring them into our organizations, and making the necessary effort to move beyond our self-imposed limitations can make a world of difference.

Over the course of thinking deeply on the topics of leadership and philosophy, I came to realize that enlightened leadership closes the gap. It promises to boost worker well-being, help them find happiness, and maximize business value, all while benefitting the leader in the process.

Whew.

	WORK CONTEXT	WORKER NEEDS	LEADERSHIP APPROACH
Higher Order	Conscious Capitalism	Self-Transcendence	Enlightened
	Knowledge/Connected	Self-Actualization	Authentic
	Post-Industrial	Esteem	Servant
	Industrial	Relationship	Transformational
	Agrarian	Safety	Transactional
Lower Order	Hunter Gatherer	Physiological	Authoritarian

Enlightened leadership is uniquely suited to produce better business results and address the Killer Bs workers—and leaders—are experiencing. When we adopt an enlightened approach, we spill its merits out into our organizations, into the world, and to the far reaches of our universe.

In the chapters that follow, we'll see the benefits that stem from the techniques I've incorporated into my Expand the

Circle enlightened leadership framework. We'll discover how the *work* improves based on studies that demonstrate the positive impact enlightened techniques can have on creativity, innovation, and productivity. We'll also see how the *workers* benefit through studies supporting claims that higher levels of engagement, well-being, mental health, and job satisfaction increase in line with elements of an enlightened approach. The beneficiaries extend well beyond the workplace. Families, communities, and society at large also benefit from enlightened leadership.

While enlightened leadership has been 2,500-plus years in the making, we must demonstrate a sense of urgency in putting it into practice. The stakes are too high and the current level of suffering too great for us to squander our precious opportunity.

As Buddhist author and teacher Jack Kornfield (1994, 39) once wrote, "The trouble is, you think you have time."

If we don't take swift action, we will remain collectively imprisoned. It breaks my heart to think that poor, outdated leadership practices are contributing to an ocean of workplace suffering every day. For the sake of our organizations and our world, we cannot delay our effort to learn and adopt an enlightened leadership approach to liberate ourselves and serve those around us.

So come, let's begin our work with the most slippery and insubordinate follower you'll ever be asked to lead:

Yourself.

PART I

THE MAP

LEAD YOURSELF

—

> *Not being able to govern events, I govern myself.*
>
> —MICHEL DE MONTAIGNE

I barely slowed down as I pulled the steering wheel hard to the right. My passenger tightened his grip on the handle above his door. Just as we careened around the corner, I slammed on the brakes. The car came to a stop at a crosswalk where a visually impaired man and his guide dog were attempting to cross.

My driver's exam wasn't going well at all.

It was my sixteenth birthday. Six months earlier, I had achieved the minimum passing score on a written exam to earn my learner's permit. I didn't practice much leading up to my road test; I thought I'd be a natural talent behind the wheel. At crunch time, I was underprepared, overanxious, and a danger to motorists and German Shepherds everywhere. During the mandatory "pull your head out" two-week waiting period, I practiced more diligently. I aced my second attempt, and I was rewarded with an operator's license and a life lesson.

In the leadership arena, there is no written exam, no road test, and no external authority to vouch for your proficiency. You must hold yourself accountable by committing yourself to study, practice, and continuous improvement. Before you can lead others, you must first learn to lead yourself.

Therefore when we first set out on the path toward enlightened leadership, we find ourselves standing alone in the Circle. Too many leaders have a fractured relationship with themselves; as they pile on more and more responsibilities, their weak foundation is likely to crumble. They may struggle with performance issues at work, health problems, and strained relationships at home. Somewhat ironically, enlightened leaders succeed by pursuing *less and less*. This means less self-doubt, self-judgment, and self-absorption. Learning to settle down and let go allows us to step into our full leadership potential.

AWARENESS

One day, a philosopher named John Perry paid a visit to the supermarket. After placing a few items into his shopping cart, he noticed a bit of spilled sugar on the floor.

"Someone is making a mess," he thought to himself (Perry 1979, 3).

He set off to find the unsuspecting shopper who must have a punctured bag of sugar in their cart. They would certainly wish to know about the mess they were making. He followed the sugar trail up and down several aisles. It eventually occurred to our philosopher that the torn bag of sugar was the one he had placed into his own cart.

"I am the one making a mess," he concluded.

Self-awareness is defined as an individual's worldview, including how they perceive themselves (Walumbwa et al. 2008). Self-awareness—and a lack thereof—is not merely the domain of bearded philosophers at the local supermarket. It affects every leader and every worker every day. Where we have self-awareness, we at least have an opportunity to make sense of what's happening to us and why. We have the chance to regulate our emotions and make intentional decisions about our thoughts and our actions.

A great deal of our self-awareness comes from what's being reflected to us from those around us. We are highly tuned to perceive and interpret cues about ourselves, often subconsciously. A slight disapproving look from a coworker tells us that our joke has pushed the boundaries too far. Nodding heads let us know that we're landing our points during a client meeting. A broad smile from the boss tells us that we're adding value and racking up points toward some future benefit. Despite this hardwired social programming, our self-awareness is not a given. For many leaders, self-awareness is often quite anemic.

Author and speaker Tasha Eurich assembled a research team to explore self-awareness. She found that self-aware people are more fulfilled, more creative, more ethical, and more promotable (Glazer 2021). Their relationships are stronger. The companies they lead are more profitable (Eurich 2017). Self-awareness, it seems, pays dividends, both figuratively and literally.

Eurich and her team conducted a remarkable study in which they found that while 95 percent of people believe they are self-aware, in reality, only 10–15 percent actually *are* self-aware. This startling discovery led Eurich to quip that "on a good day, 80 percent of us are lying to ourselves about whether we're lying to ourselves" (Eurich 2017).

Over the course of her research, Eurich concluded that self-awareness can be divided into two components, both of which are critical to success. The first is internal self-awareness, or how clearly we see ourselves. The second is external self-awareness, or how clearly we see how others perceive us.

When each dimension is divided into either a high or a low degree of awareness, a fascinating two-by-two grid emerges. Individuals who are found to be high on both components are considered "Aware." Those who rate as low on both are characterized as "Seekers."

The remaining two categories are where things really get interesting.

An individual with high internal self-awareness but low external self-awareness is referred to as an "Introspector." Partial credit goes to these individuals, but so does a higher likelihood of being blindsided when they run afoul of another person's perception of them. "What do you mean that I'm not forceful enough with my direct reports? I had no idea you felt that way."

An individual who is low on internal self-awareness but high on external self-awareness is a "Pleaser." Again, partial credit comes with a side helping of caution. Pleasers may be so fixated on how others perceive them that they may fail to make decisions based on what *they* want. They may focus so heavily on what makes others happy that they fail to acknowledge— or perhaps even realize—what would make *them* happy.

Lacking self-awareness, how many leaders do you know who run up and down the halls spilling sugar as they go? I know I have on more than one occasion. Raising our awareness, therefore, requires that we put ourselves under a microscope. Ironically, we need to borrow others' eyes to fully see ourselves.

Creating awareness, encouraging personal discovery, and being a "loving critic" are key functions of an executive coach. When working alongside leaders, professional coaches bring objectivity to the coaching process, and they have access to a variety of tools that can help leaders explore our deepest held values, strengths, anxieties, and more. A big part of a coach's job is referred to as "holding up a mirror" so we can see ourselves just a bit more clearly.

A big part of our role as leaders is to share our observations and insights with others, yet we may neglect our own opportunities to do the same for ourselves. This oversight can easily seep into our leadership. In his book *Coaching for Performance: GROWing Human Potential and Purpose—The Principles and Practice of Coaching and Leadership*, the late, great coaching legend Sir John Whitmore (2009, 50) cautions us that, "Our own psychological history and prejudices—and no one is free of either—will influence our communication." Forewarned, it seems, is forearmed.

A considerable body of research supports the relationship between self-awareness and desirable outcomes in our workplaces. In one study, accurately self-aware leaders had subordinates who evaluated them as better leaders and experienced higher levels of job satisfaction themselves (Moshavi, Brown, and Dodd 2003). These results stood in stark contrast to those produced by other leaders who overestimated their self-awareness.

A leader's self-awareness and the authentic leadership that flow from it have been positively connected to trust, commitment, engagement, and performance on the part of followers (Einola and Alvesson 2021). It's also encouraging to note that as leaders become more self-aware, they invite their followers to increase their own leadership capabilities in kind (Bracht et al. 2021).

Which brings us back to the supermarket.

Being a philosopher, the sugar-spilling John Perry thought deeply about his experience. He noted that upon realizing that he was the one making the mess, his beliefs about himself and his context changed. This shift is what permitted him to change his behavior—in his case, to stop making a mess. For those of us less-than-perfect leaders, it's highly encouraging to know that we can raise our self-awareness, modify our beliefs, and improve our behaviors to elevate our leadership ability.

ACCEPTANCE

At the northernmost tip of the Colorado River stands an imposing curved mountain of smooth concrete. The Hoover Dam towers sixty stories high and weighs over 6,600,000 tons. More than 21,000 workers toiled away on its construction over four years during the heart of the Great Depression (National Parks Service, n.d.).

The base of the dam is as thick as two football fields. Its gargantuan walls hold back Lake Mead, the largest man-made reservoir in the United States. This sheet of concrete withstands 45,000 pounds of pressure per square foot because of the massive volume of water in the reservoir (USBR, n.d.).

As leaders, we too know the strain of holding back. When we become aware of a personal shortcoming or recognize that we have a personality trait that we're not altogether proud of, we quickly try to cover it up. We erect a wall between those around us and the unfiltered version of ourselves. To prevent less favorable aspects of ourselves from spilling out, we reinforce the dam without recognizing the potential consequences.

Self-acceptance, by contrast, refers to a willingness to not only acknowledge but to embrace one's limitations and shortcomings. While our natural tendency may be to downplay or cover up our perceived weaknesses, doing so not only creates a host of mental maladies but also leads to a missed opportunity to deepen our leadership.

Steven C. Hayes is a clinical psychologist and an educator. As a young psychology professor, Hayes was caught in a vicious cycle. He was eager to prove himself and make his contribution as a part of the faculty (Hayes 2020). During a department meeting, the more senior professors began to argue. As the volume and tension of their discussion rose, so did the intensity Hayes felt bubbling up inside. That's when he experienced his first panic attack. He raised his hand, but when all eyes turned to him, he found that he was unable to speak—not a single word.

Mortified, Hayes scrambled out of the room. In the years that followed, he went to great lengths to try to control his anxiety. He developed a series of coping mechanisms to bottle up and overpower his emotions, but to no avail. Being a professor of psychology, his ailment was all the more troublesome and embarrassing.

One night, while at home, Hayes experienced tightness in his arm. He initially thought he was having a heart attack. As he thought more deeply about what he was experiencing and his long history of roiling anxiety, he determined that he was having a panic attack. His runaway thoughts were once again getting the better of him. Being anxious about his anxiety had completely dominated his life at that point, and now he felt as if he were on the brink of death.

On that night, Hayes hit rock bottom. He let out a loud, primal scream borne of the hopelessness that he felt. In doing so, he hit on a way out.

Hayes came to a series of realizations that night. First, he was not merely the content of his thoughts. Sure, he had thoughts—often pressing, anxious thoughts—but these were separate from the construct he experienced as his sense of self. Second, no matter how disturbing his thoughts may have been, he was able to observe them from an independent vantage point. Finally, he realized that he had long been avoiding painful experiences and attempting to control any situation that he thought might produce negative emotions.

As a clinical psychologist, Hayes had a unique opportunity to not only help himself but to liberate others who suffered from similar mental afflictions. After reflecting upon his realizations from that night, he took his first tentative steps on a path to wellness and recovery. He parlayed his experience and insight into a new therapeutic approach called Acceptance and Commitment Therapy (ACT). Today, acceptance is one of six core practices in the ACT methodology.

Rather than turn away from negative thoughts and emotions, ACT encourages us to turn toward them. Hayes defines acceptance as "the full embrace of our personal experience in an empowered, not in a victimized state" (Hayes 2020, 21). The way we approach our negative thoughts and emotions, therefore, is more important than their content.

Acceptance involves shifting from avoiding negative experiences to appreciating them (Sounds True 2020). By observing our thought processes as they unfold, we can give ourselves the space we need to not be carried away by them. According to Hayes, over the course of our personal histories, even those negative aspects of ourselves and the challenging experiences we've endured hold lessons if we can find the courage to take advantage of them.

Hayes observes, "Inside your suffering, you find the capacity to love yourself in a different way." We can each resist any futile temptation of exerting control over our experiences in favor of a more constructive mindset and approach, even when things aren't altogether pleasant. Pain, loss, and impermanence are a natural part of life. Hayes has seen firsthand that when you accept the lesson and the gift inside your pain, you can move toward what you care about most.

As Hayes's experience demonstrates, rather than attempting to hold back painful experiences Hoover Dam-style, we need to open ourselves to the lessons they hold. This is what's implied by the adage "no pain, no change." Bestselling author, speaker, and researcher Brené Brown left no white space between growth and acceptance when she told podcast host Tim Ferriss, "I don't think you can truly change for the better in a lasting, meaningful way unless it is driven by self-acceptance" (Ferriss 2020).

For leaders, this type of personal growth is healthy and necessary, but limits exist. Should we be expected to whittle away all our faults? Should we press ourselves headlong toward our personal definition of what it means to be a perfect leader?

Mari Ruti is an authority on character development and a professor at the University of Toronto, where her tantalizingly eclectic research interests include philosophy, psychoanalysis, culture, trauma, gender, and sexuality. In her book *The Call of Character: Living a Life Worth Living,* Ruti (2014) explores a concept she calls "self-surrender." This involves accepting all parts of ourselves and not just the comfortable bits we choose to expose to others.

Ruti (2014, 123) writes that "self-surrender can be an essential component of self-fashioning." Most of our energy goes into constructing and continuously shoring up and defending carefully curated aspects of our identity. But for Ruti, character is not solely the result of a calculated process and a well-executed act of creation. She urges us to "suspend the relatively organized structure of our identity by letting ourselves fall into a less organized state of being." Her counsel is that we allow some aspects of our innermost selves—including our imperfections—to naturally bubble to the surface.

Strong evidence exists that our mental wellness will improve if we're able to accomplish this. Dr. Albert Ellis is a legendary psychologist who was a leading proponent of a construct known as unconditional self-acceptance. Those of us who can make lasting peace with the totality of our self-perception are more likely to "avoid the common pitfall of failing to live up to our (often unrealistic) expectations and the consequent feelings of self-denigration, low self-esteem, and depression" (Levinson 2007).

Organizational studies have also found a positive relationship between leaders' degree of self-acceptance and their effectiveness (Denmark 1973). In fact, as a leader, your willingness to demonstrate humility opens a door to your followers. Research has shown that leader humility serves as a positive model that is relatable to followers who face similar uncertainty and self-doubt. Self-acceptance and self-disclosure can spill over and benefit others if we let them (Owens and Hekman 2012).

The Hoover Dam was purposefully engineered to hold back the waters of Lake Mead to protect tens of thousands of residents and acres of farmland along the river. As leaders, we weren't built to endure that type of constant strain. When we hold back our perceived faults and negative feelings, we often do so out of self-preservation and self-interest. We seek to control our circumstances and prevent negative outcomes. Just as Hayes experienced, we run the risk of reaching catastrophic failure like a dam on the brink of bursting.

Self-acceptance is about appreciating the totality of our human experience and what makes us uniquely suited—positively and negatively—to the leadership moment. Acceptance can become a source of personal power and increased leadership capacity if we embrace it.

CONFIDENCE

You rock back and forth, twirling the tennis racket in your hand. You're about to be on the receiving end of a 125-mile-per-hour overhand serve. You're trying to visualize a successful return stroke, but mostly you're hoping the ball doesn't hit you in the face. You're racked with self-doubt, wondering if you're really up to this. You're squared off against Serena Williams, winner of twenty-three Grand Slam tennis titles. She's one of the most powerful athletes in US history, so your lack of confidence should come as no surprise.

Any lack of confidence on her part—even against a real-life opponent—is downright shocking.

Williams found herself trailing after the opening set in a 2020 French Open match against an opponent ranked one hundred places lower than her at the time. After collecting herself, Williams rallied to win the match. Afterward, when asked about the turnaround, she said, "The biggest difference was just confidence. I just needed to play with more confidence, like I'm Serena" (Addicott 2020). Despite her athletic prowess, self-confidence wasn't automatic for Williams. "It was definitely something I had to work on; it did not come naturally at all," she later reflected (Campbell 2022).

Self-confidence is all about expectations. If you expect to be successful, you're more likely to expend the effort it takes to achieve your goals (Kanter 2005). Self-confidence has two basic dimensions (Axelrod 2017). The first is generalized—essentially an enduring personality trait. The second is specific to the task at hand. Both show up in the attitude we bring to our leadership. Are we confident that we'll succeed no matter the situation?

Self-confidence is a personal judgment and can only be determined by the individual. Nobody can *make* you or anybody else more or less self-confident. This means that when it comes to confidence, you're holding serve.

"Confidence is the necessary spark before everything that follows," according to educator and activist Brittany Packnett Cunningham (2019). In a moving talk, Cunningham shared that she recognized the importance of confidence early in her childhood, and her fascination with the topic persists to this day. She describes confidence as "the most important journey of my life, a journey that, to be honest, I'm still on."

As a teacher, Cunningham realized that she had the capacity to stoke the flames of a child's self-confidence or snuff them out entirely. We find ourselves in both positions as leaders. Our confidence is influenced by the attitudes and behaviors of our managers, peers, and even our direct reports. The latter group is most under our own influence. A thoughtful shout-out for a job well done can feed a subordinate's self-confidence. A loose negative comment in a moment of frustration or weakness on our part can deal a lingering blow to the same individual's mindset.

Self-confidence fuels another critical attribute of leadership: self-esteem. While confidence is a personal judgment regarding expectations and likelihood of success, self-esteem relates to one's personal sense of worth. As we'll soon see, both are critical to a leader's performance.

Simone Alicia is known as "The Self Esteem Doctor." As a fashion model, Alicia took an interest in how children regarded her and her fellow models as being supremely confident. She knew better. Many models suffered from massive bouts of self-doubt; under the bright lights and the snapping camera shutters, they were actors playing a part. Alicia made a critical connection, and she now teaches confidence in the classroom to help young people establish a solid foundation.

She observes that self-esteem is central to the way we make decisions as well as our own self-image—what we're capable of accomplishing and why (Samadi 2021). In an interview, Alicia told me, "Self-esteem is the way we think about ourselves and our lives. This definition puts the power in our hands." Despite its beneficial role in so many life domains, there can be a backlash against people who demonstrate confidence. She chalks much of this up to societal pressures. "There's this massive misconception that being proud of yourself is somehow arrogance." The crowd, it seems, has ways of pulling others back to what it perceives as its acceptable average.

Despite the downward pressure, leaders must understand and honor the links in the chain. Confidence begets esteem which begets competence. A leader who has self-confidence but who lacks self-esteem eventually will find that their leadership rings hollow. Without self-confidence, self-esteem is unattainable. This is a big reason why Cunningham referred to confidence as a "necessary spark," and why it's so important to develop and protect it.

When the self-confidence of children—and first-time leaders—comes under fire, it can sow the seeds of a lifetime of hesitation and self-limiting beliefs. I see this happen all the time regarding early career promotions. Whenever a star performer begins to set themselves apart from their peers, they're often considered for a management position. "If she's that good," the logic goes, "think about how much better performance we'll get from the team if we put her in charge!"

Immediately, a few things happen. First, the previously confident star performer now experiences something new: self-doubt. Second, the shiny new manager feels awkward directing the activities of individuals who were her coworkers the day before. Right when she's at her most vulnerable, she's forced to navigate a highly complex social and organizational situation. She's on her heels, and the shots are whizzing by her head faster than a Serena Williams forehand smash.

When it comes to self-confidence in our leadership, research suggests that a "just right" Goldilocks approach is the sweet spot. In one study, researchers found that supervisors who lacked confidence in their leadership ability were more likely to address management problems using passive techniques such as referring matters to a superior or involving human resources (Kipnis and Lane 1962). These passive responses diminished the leader's authority and increased administrative costs. A leader's confidence has an upper limit, however. An overconfident leader can invite risk to themselves, their teams, and their organization (Moore 2021). One reason for this is that overconfidence may cause the leader to put less effort into preparation and risk mitigation. Each of us needs to dial in the "just right" amount of self-confidence. We can only do this for ourselves.

Which takes us back inside the lines staring down a 125-mile-per-hour serve.

Serena Williams has identified the chief cause of her occasional confidence issues; she's a perfectionist. "I have put so much perfection into my habits that if it's not perfect, then it's not enough for me" (Addicott 2020). To her credit, Williams recognized that this tendency carries a more significant consequence than her short-term performance. She's a role model to those who look up to her, after all. In a *Fortune* essay coinciding with International Women's Day, Williams (2019) wrote, "I want to make it clear that perfection is an impossible goal and should never be a true pursuit in life."

In showing both vulnerability and accountability, Williams demonstrates what every leader must come to understand; confidence and leadership go hand in hand.

AUTHENTICITY

The market for fine art paintings has grown white-hot in recent years. Part of the appeal of rare paintings is the master craft they display. Another is their rarity; they just don't make them like they used to. The world-class auction house Sotheby's once sold a portrait by Frans Hals for 8.5 million pounds and a Parmigianino oil painting for $842,500 (Subramanian 2018). Tidy sums, to be sure, but there's just one problem; they were fakes.

The forgeries were detected by Jamie Martin, a forensic art investigator. Considering the high stakes surrounding his verdicts, Martin has been enlisted by the FBI, made an appearance on the television news program *60 Minutes*, and is now employed by Sotheby's. He's been referred to as "a rock star in his field" (Bonenti 2022). He was drawn to this unique line of work in search of the truth. "I like living within the four corners of what's right and what's wrong," he said (Subramanian 2018). On the basis of Martin's judgment, a work of art can instantly go from priceless to worthless.

Leaders who eschew authenticity face the same risk.

To help him separate the seemingly real from the almost certainly fake, Martin relies on an exacting nature, a keen eye, and sophisticated tools of detection. People who observe leaders in action rarely have any of these assets, but they can spot inauthentic leadership all the same. Humans are social animals, and we're wired to pick up on even the most subtle cues. Even minor inconsistencies between what a leader says and their actions can stick out like a misspelled signature on a fine art fake. A lack of authenticity reduces follower trust, commitment, and effort. Here too, the stakes are high.

In the leadership domain, authenticity is the result of discovering one's purpose or personal mission, living in line with one's values, experiencing deep connection in relationships at work and beyond it, and exercising self-regulation to stay on course when it's ever so tempting to deviate. Becoming an authentic leader requires careful self-examination and making tough choices to hone in on what most truly defines you.

Martha Beck is a bestselling author and a Harvard-trained sociologist. Beck has written extensively about authenticity, what it means to be whole, and what happens when we're able to bring our full and genuine selves to our lives and the world around us. In her book *The Way of Integrity: Finding the Path to Your True Self,* she writes, "When you experience unity of intention, fascination, and purpose, you live like a bloodhound on a scent, joyfully doing what feels truest in each moment" (Beck 2021).

Beck's use of the term *integrity* speaks to its sense of structural soundness rather than its moral connotation. She notes that the word integrity is derived from the Latin word *integer,* or "one thing whole and undivided" (Berman 2021). This definition issues a challenge to aspiring authentic leaders. Demonstrating attitudes, values, and behaviors in line with our truest selves is not enough. As leaders, we must go further and strive to bring our full capacity into our leadership.

One of my most formative leadership experiences taught me how *not* to lead. It came early in my military service, while I was at Fort Benning, Georgia, for parachute training. Cadets and service members from all branches of the military endured one-hundred-degree days and short nights before completing a qualifying series of five static line parachute jumps. Between exercises, we were broken into smaller four-person teams to study, drill, and prepare for the next period of instruction.

I was the senior enlisted person in my group, so I was the de facto supervisor. Having no real leadership experience, I asked myself how other Marines leaders might comport themselves in my situation.

I was gruff. I was serious. I was profane.

Basically, I wasn't myself at all. I was ineffective and uncomfortable as a result. I immediately recognized my mistake. It was as if I were wearing a jacket that was too small. I had tried to cover up my natural leadership style.

I am warm. I am jovial. I am profane.

When I began to lead from a position of authenticity, I immediately felt lighter. My leadership flowed more naturally, and I gradually came to learn that there was no need to try and be something I'm not or plaster over my perceived idiosyncrasies.

While I'm no Rembrandt, I studied our craft of leadership and improved my brushstrokes all the same. I leaned into my most authentic attributes, including enthusiasm, empathy, compassion, and humor. I brought more of my unique self into my leadership. These were important steps on my path toward becoming an authentic leader.

An authentic leadership style integrates a high level of self-awareness, a genuine relationship with oneself and others, and behavior aligned with one's personal worldview and morals (Optimizing 2022). Authentic leadership has been found to increase follower trust, well-being, commitment, engagement, and performance (Einola and Alvesson 2021). As a result, an authentic leadership approach reduces the likelihood of turnover, burnout, and counterproductive work behaviors. In one study, authenticity garnered trust among followers and a subsequent trickle-down flow through progressive levels of engagement, task performance, and coworker relationships (Lusianingrum and Santoso 2022). Authentic leadership has even been shown to boost creativity (Ribiero, Duarte and Filipe 2018).

This begs the question: if authentic leadership is so powerful, why do so many leaders find it elusive just as I once had?

Part of the reason is because the imitation game is as tempting in the leadership domain as it is in the world of fine art. Truly knowing and accepting yourself takes time, and putting yourself fully into the world takes courage. As a result, many leaders think about which types of attitudes and behaviors they *should* project and then they try to mimic these brushstrokes.

They may get away with it for a while, but a keen eye could see through the facade at any moment. Forensic art examiner Jamie Martin offers this tongue-in-cheek advice to would-be art forgers: "Never wear synthetic fibers while making a forgery" (Gates 2018). Authentic leadership scholar Bill George offers similar advice to would-be leadership forgers: "You cannot 'fake it till you make it' by putting on a show as a leader or being a chameleon in your style" (George 2015). The path to authenticity is therefore: be yourself and be *fully* yourself.

Once you're able to grasp your full and authentic self, you'll be ready to let it all go.

TRANSCENDENCE

Chances are you'd heard of Abraham Maslow and his pyramid-shaped hierarchy of needs well before picking up this book. His framework has been called "one of the most cognitively contagious ideas in the behavioral sciences" (Kenrick et al. 2010). It's elegantly simple, and it's highly relatable. I know that if I were exceptionally hungry, I'd be much more interested in a slice of pizza than in refreshing a relationship with a long-lost coworker. However, most people don't know something about his famous framework.

It's incomplete.

The tippy top of the pyramid Maslow first developed in 1943 most often lists self-actualization, a peak state of human experience similar to Beck's structural integrity. This is a state where one realizes one's full potential. As Maslow continued his study of self-actualized individuals and their peak experiences, however, he became interested in how often they shared having *transcendent* experiences. These are times when they felt a deep sense of identity and engagement with something bigger than themselves, whether it be selfless service to other human beings, a meditative mindfulness, or a profound connection to the universe (Koltko-Rivera 2006).

This presents a paradox to self-improvement junkies and aspiring leaders alike. Investment in oneself naturally culminates in a desire to go beyond this type of self-directed pursuit toward an all-consuming effort to support other people or causes (Worth and Smith 2021).

Soon after he documented his popular hierarchy, Maslow became uncomfortable with the field's undue focus on only its ego-centric aspects. He later described self-transcendence as an ability for an individual to achieve an integrated consciousness with other humans (Maslow 1968). Owing in part to its religious or spiritual connotation, the psychology literature failed to pick up his later extensions of the needs framework with the same zeal. Yet fully embracing the draw of self-transcendence may increase our understanding of our intrinsic drives and behaviors (Koltko-Rivera 2006). Doing so is every bit as essential to enlightened leadership.

Around the same time that Maslow was popularizing his hierarchy and pondering its limitations, an Austrian psychiatrist half a world away was living its implications.

Viktor Frankl was arrested by the Nazis in 1942 and deported along with his wife and parents to Terezín Ghetto north of Prague (Viktor Frankl Institute, n.d.). Frankl would spend the next three years in various concentration camps. As a trained neurologist and existential thinker, Frankl sought to ease the mental suffering and anguish of his fellow prisoners while also thinking deeply about the meaning of life. He later observed that the prisoners who were able to hold on to something in their life that made it meaningful were able to survive the atrocities, while those who fell into hopelessness and despair did not (Frankl et al. 2015). This led Frankl to the conclusion that "those who have a 'why' to live, can bear with almost any 'how.'"

After being freed from the Türkheim camp in 1945, Frankl continued to practice, write, and speak about humanistic psychology and existential meaning. Like Maslow, he espoused the role and value of self-transcendence. He wrote that "being human profoundly means being open to the world, a world, that is, replete with other beings to encounter and with meanings to fulfill" (Frankl 1966, 97). In fact, he considered this egoless tendency to be an essential human quality. According to Frankl (1966, 104), "Human existence is not authentic unless it is lived in terms of self-transcendence."

The need for self-transcendence has clear implications for leaders at every level. Maslow's observation that an ego-only pursuit is a dead end echoes the reflections of countless CEOs and business leaders who have reached the height of success or the end of their professional journey. They speak most often of the strength of the relationships they developed and having been a part of something special. They rarely celebrate the accolades they achieved and the material spoils they collected along the way.

Likewise, Frankl's observation that the world is full of other people seeking their own meaning certainly reflects what is happening in our organizations and among our closest contacts at this very moment. Each of us leaders—from the most senior to the most inexperienced individual contributor—is surrounded by others who need us to be willing to concern ourselves with their needs as much as we do our own.

Recall the three Killer Bs. We each have a need for being, belonging, and something bigger than ourselves. They pose existential questions to each of us. Who am I really? Where do I fit in? How does what I'm doing make a difference in the world?

These questions we each experience are not merely convenient to consider; we must reconcile them to realize our full leadership potential. In his book *One Unbounded Ocean of Consciousness: Simple Answers to The Big Questions in Life*, Harvard-trained neuroscientist Tony Nader (2021) highlights the importance of these deeply rooted existential questions. He writes that our beliefs about our integral purpose and meaning "shape our lives as foundations of our thinking, feeling, and behaving." As leaders, we can't whisk away these "unanswerable" questions or convince ourselves that we can tend to them once our schedules permit.

Like Maslow's partial pyramid, however, answering these questions merely from our own perspective is incomplete. After dedicating significant attention and effort to develop our awareness, accept the totality of our strengths and shortcomings, build our confidence, and embrace our authentic selves, we're asked to do the unthinkable. We're asked to *stop* thinking of ourselves.

Nader defines the term *transcend* as "to go beyond" (Gervais 2021). If we're going to channel the full force of our leadership, we must Expand the Circle and go beyond our ego-constrained confines. In doing so, we make ourselves ready to take the next step in our enlightened leadership journey. We are ready to turn our attention toward leading others.

* * *

TIPS & TAKEAWAYS

1. **Begin at the beginning.** Before you can effectively lead others, you must learn to lead yourself. While it may be tempting to skip steps, invest in personal reflection and self-mastery to deepen your leadership capacity.

2. **Know thyself.** An enlightened leader is a self-aware leader. Examine your personal values, guiding beliefs, strengths, limitations, and your motivation to lead. Make checking in with yourself a regular habit.

3. **Give yourself grace.** Remember that no leader is perfect. Rather than hide away your perceived flaws, accept that they're an essential part of you. Learn from your setbacks and your shortcomings.

4. **Be bold.** Confidence comes from the expectation that you will succeed. Build on that foundation by appreciating the value you create as a leader. Remember that self-confidence and self-esteem precede competence.

5. **Be yourself and be fully yourself.** Strive to exhibit the values, attitudes, and behaviors that align with your most authentic self. Don't play small; find the courage and the creativity to bring all of yourself into your leadership.

6. **Think bigger.** After investing heavily in personal awareness, insight, and action, be prepared to let it all go. Your willingness to transcend self-absorption and self-limiting boundaries will unlock your next leadership level.

LEAD OTHERS

———

You manage things; you lead people.

—GRACE MURRAY HOPPER

Our mission was clear: navigate the densely wooded mountainside, avoid our captors, and reach the safe house several miles away. We had already spent several days learning how to fashion a splint out of tree branches, create a makeshift shelter from a parachute, and forage for food. Such is life at SERE School, short for Survive, Evade, Resist, Escape—four critical activities at the prisoner of war simulation camp situated in Brunswick, Maine.

Our group broke into pairs. My assigned partner was a US Navy lieutenant trained as an F-14 Tomcat fighter pilot. Despite being an officer and my superior, he knew he was out of his element.

"You're the Marine. Lead the way." He jammed the map into my hand and elbowed me forward.

"Aye, sir." I swallowed hard and tried to hide my nervousness.

Over several tense hours, we climbed, darted, and hid. I kept him on my hip at all times. On a few occasions, we heard our mock captors firing faux weapons and shouting as they gobbled up our classmates. I had us moving well, but we were running out of time.

After a final check of the map, I pointed toward a clearing. As we crept forward, Top Gun and I exchanged silent nods. We were either about to be captured or . . .

"Congratulations!" a uniformed Navy instructor shouted. "You made it."

Inside the safe house, we were rewarded with hot meals and an extra hour of downtime. Soon we would be collected as "war criminals" and taken to our cells for the next phase of our training. The Lieutenant and I took full advantage of our well-earned respite while we could. I could sense him staring at me over his steaming cup of soup. He smiled with a toothy grin.

"Holy shit. You did it, Marine." he chuckled.

"*We* did it, sir." After what we had just been through, I felt comfortable correcting him.

When we Expand the Circle beyond ourselves alone, we arrive at our relationships with Others. That relationship may be with a direct report, a peer, or a senior manager. In any of our one-on-one relationships, failing to embrace an enlightened leadership approach creates a distance between us. Closing that gap allows us to amplify the combined effect of our leadership and both parties' success and welfare in the process.

EMPATHY

Most of us have felt the urge to help a friend in need, but where does this feeling come from, and are there limits to how strongly we feel it? To shed light on these questions, Inbal Ben-Ami Bartal and a team of researchers from the University of Chicago conducted a series of experiments to study the helping motivation and behaviors of rats (Ben-Ami Bartal et al. 2014). The scientists constructed a large cage and placed a laboratory rat inside. In the center of the cage, they installed a clear tube featuring a latched door the helper rat could open if it were so inclined.

In experiments where the tube was empty or whenever it contained a toy rat as its prisoner, the helper paid the tube no attention whatsoever. In trials where a second rat was loaded into the tube, each helper sprung its buddy so the two could frolic about the cage together.

The scheming scientists decided to up the stakes. They added a second tube that contained some delicious chocolate chips. Surely the rat would prefer the snack instead of releasing its buddy. Surprisingly, over a series of trials with different test subjects, the rats all opted to save their buddies and share the snacks, even if some hesitant heroes consumed roughly half the morsels before releasing their companions. The motivation to help another rat in distress universally proved stronger than each helper's sweet tooth.

"That was very compelling," explained researcher Peggy Mason. "It said to us that essentially helping their cage mate is on a par with chocolate. He can hog the entire chocolate stash if he wanted to. And he does not. We were shocked" (Wein 2015).

I wasn't shocked. I was once trapped like a rat.

I was a shy kid growing up, and when I began first grade, I sat under a yellow jungle gym each recess period and cried. I couldn't bring myself to approach any of the other boys before they dashed off to play soccer in the fields behind the school. After a few days of this, a classmate named Dave approached me as I sat on the ground with my head in my hands. He said, "Hey—wanna come play?"

Did I ever! I jumped to my feet, and we ran off to the soccer fields. That day, Dave and I began a friendship that would carry us from elementary school through becoming college roommates. This was one of my earliest experiences of peer leadership, and it left quite an impression on me. In that moment under the jungle gym, Dave *saw* me, and he felt my distress.

It turns out that not only do first graders like Dave have an ability to intuit what others are likely feeling, but it's a cognitive skill they've had for quite some time.

A small curtain opens to reveal a simplistic puppet show set with a modest hill at its center. A puppeteer dangles a yellow circle and slowly enacts a scene for a solitary audience member. The yellow circle slowly makes its way up the hill.

Suddenly, a three-dimensional red triangle emerges at the top of the hill and pushes the circle back to the bottom. The mean red triangle quickly ascends the hill and disappears out of view. After suffering the injustice, the yellow circle resumes its climb. This time, a friendly green cube appears at the bottom of the hill, and it helps nudge the circle to the top.

This may seem like the least interesting puppet show in the history of puppet shows, but its six-month-old audience member was paying very careful attention. The puppet show was put on by a research team from the Cognition Center at Yale University. The highly educated puppeteers constructed the experiment to study the moral life of babies (Bloom 2010).

After the show's dramatic action came to its climax, an experimenter brought the adorable research subject a tray holding the red triangle and green cube from the puppet show. The scientists wanted to observe which toy a sample of infants would prefer after watching the performance. The babies overwhelmingly reached for the helpful cube rather than the hindering triangle. Having witnessed the circle's joys and frustrations while it attempted to climb the hill, it's as if each baby was saying, "I feel your pain, Mr. Circle, and I shall not be playing with that mean Mr. Triangle."

Considering the empathic capacity of rats and babies, it's fair to presume that leaders also have this capability. Helen Riess is an associate clinical professor of psychiatry at Harvard Medical School and the author of *The Empathy Effect: Seven Neuroscience-Based Keys for Transforming the Way We Live, Love, Work, and Connect Across Differences*. She explains, "We are all connected on a neurobiological level far more than we have previously realized. Consciously or not, we are in constant, natural resonance with one another's feelings. When we are engaged in shared mind awareness, the possibilities for mutual aid and collaborative problem solving abound" (Riess and Neporent 2018).

Leaders take heed. Your executive leadership teams and your followers are paying attention. The Center for Creative Leadership found that managers whose bosses consider them to be empathetic are also viewed as better performers. The same is true for those managers having subordinates who rate them highly for empathy. These admired leaders were similarly evaluated as high performers by their bosses (Leading Effectively 2020).

Empathy has been linked to higher levels of productivity, work-life balance, and having positive work experiences. Workers who consider their managers to be empathetic display higher levels of innovation and employee engagement as compared to those having less empathetic managers. Diversity, inclusion, and intent to stay have each been linked to supervisors having higher levels of empathy (Van Bommel 2021). Empathy is good for your people, good for your career prospects, and good for your business.

Unfortunately, empathy in the workplace is often undermined by several all too common factors. I've seen a variety of empathy derailers including stress, fatigue, anxiety, and a drive to produce results that outweighs employee welfare. These afflictions can erode a leader's attention to the experiences and distress of those around them; this can happen when the leader's focus and energy get monopolized by their own needs and interests. Fortunately, with sufficient awareness and practice, empathy can be developed and sustained, even during trying times.

Empathy is a prerequisite to leading others. If we couldn't sense and internalize what other people are feeling, we would have no motivation or ability to help them. Fortunately, empathy has a neurobiological basis; it's literally wired into our brains. According to Riess, "Humans are made to get this feeling to motivate them to do something to help" (Heal the Divide 2020).

Recall our helper rat who sprung its cage mate. To paraphrase Humphrey Bogart's legendary line in *Casablanca*, I think empathy is the beginning of a beautiful friendship. But for that friendship to materialize, a leader's empathetic motivation has to be converted into action.

ALTRUISM

In 2009, a BBC film crew was conducting operations in the chilly waters near Antarctica. While sailing, and presumably while shivering, the group observed a pod of killer whales harassing a pair of humpback whales. While killer whales don't pose much of a threat to the considerably larger humpbacks, this particular killer whale pod was quite agitated. It had taken an interest in a seal that was hiding in the humpbacks' general vicinity.

When the seal swam away, the killer whales gave chase. One of the humpbacks maneuvered underneath the seal, rolled onto its back, and positioned the seal on its massive belly.

The seal began to slide off, but the humpback used its flipper like a giant pinball paddle, and it nudged the seal back to the center of its chest. "No seal for you!"

Robert Pitman, now a marine ecologist for the National Oceanic and Atmospheric Administration (NOAA) Fisheries, was with the BBC film crew during the exchange. When he later discussed the behavior he had witnessed with his colleagues around the world, Pitman discovered that there had been several observations of this humpback behavior. This had not been a random or accidental act, but rather a repeatedly observed form of interspecies altruism.

After studying similar incidents, scientists now know that if humpbacks sense an animal in distress, they're likely to issue an audible attack call. They rally their massive pals to swim directly into a pod of killer whales to break up their aggressive act. "What they want to do is protect whatever it is [the killer whales] are attacking," Pitman explained (Marine Mammal 2021).

Even if the killer whales don't pose a direct threat to the humpbacks, energy preserves are scarce, and they could still be injured in a melee. Acting is costly and could be risky for the humpbacks, so why do they choose to intervene?

A life-changing experience led one nineteen-year-old to investigate this very question as it pertains to altruistic humans.

Abigail Marsh was driving along the freeway one night en route to her home in Tacoma, Washington, when a dog darted out in front of her car (Marsh 2016). She slammed on the brakes. Her car fishtailed, spun around, and came to a stop in the passing lane facing backward. Making matters worse, the car had stalled. Marsh was certain she was about to die.

To her surprise, a stranger pulled over on the side of the freeway. He got out of his vehicle and ran across four lanes of oncoming traffic to reach her. He helped her get the car started again and navigated her to the side of the road and to safety. Before she could learn his name or even say thank you, he drove away.

After her harrowing experience, Marsh went on to study altruism and the human capacity to care for others. Marsh later became the head of Georgetown University's Laboratory of Social and Affective Neuroscience. While conducting her research, she constructed this definition of altruism: "a voluntary, costly behavior motivated by the desire to help another individual."

Marsh developed her insights in part by studying two altruistically opposed groups of individuals: kidney donors and psychopaths. She discovered that fear plays a significant mediating role in altruistic behavior. At these extremes, she discovered that the type of person who would donate a kidney to a stranger is motivated to perform such a significant act of kindness in part due to their being highly sensitive to others' fear. By contrast, an inability to feel others' fear contributes to psychopathic behavior (Nutt 2021).

If humpback whales, roadside Samaritans, and kidney donors are all capable of altruistic acts, what's possible for us leaders?

In 1970, Robert K. Greenleaf began to write essays introducing the topic of servant leadership. He encouraged leaders to hold a primary goal of serving their followers in a selfless, empathic, and altruistic fashion. According to Greenleaf, this type of leader seeks to "make sure that other people's highest priority needs are being served" (Greenleaf et al. 2002). While offering this counsel, it wasn't lost on Greenleaf that this course of action costs the servant-leader a great deal of effort and exposes them to some degree of risk. What if you try to take a servant-first approach but you aren't certain that doing so will produce the desired result for the follower, for the enterprise, or for yourself as the leader? Greenleaf's response was succinct. "This is part of the human dilemma; one cannot know for sure."

Fortunately, several studies tilt the scale in favor of empathetic servant leadership. A research team conducted a survey of more than 1,500 workers representing organizations from around the globe (Prime and Salib 2014). Respondents were asked to share their work experiences related to the altruistic styles of their managers. Workers who responded affirmatively to having an altruistic manager were more likely to feel included on their respective teams and were observed to be more innovative. These workers also went above and beyond what was required of them by demonstrating altruistic behaviors themselves. For example, they were more likely to take on responsibilities for colleagues who were sick or absent. Like empathy, altruism is good for people, leaders, and the business.

Leadership is about producing results with and through other people. Inevitably the "through other people" part of the leadership equation is going to cost you, and there's no guarantee that you'll be successful in your aim. What you'll find, however, is that the investment is well worth the effort and inherent risks. Altruistic leaders who act on their impulse to help those around them can amplify their impact. They're better able to marshal and direct the efforts of others in pursuit of a collective goal.

Like a workplace equivalent of a mighty humpback whale, if you feel empathy toward others and if you're willing to act on your altruistic intentions, you will double your leadership impact. You will benefit the other person through your support, and your actions will elevate your circumstances in kind.

TRUST

Stephen M. R. Covey is a crown prince in the leadership field. His father, Stephen R. Covey, was the celebrated author of *The 7 Habits of Highly Effective People*, one of the most influential leadership and personal development books of all time. After developing the strategy that helped support his father's book launch, Covey orchestrated a merger with the prominent leadership consultancy Franklin Quest. Today, FranklinCovey is one of the largest leadership development companies in the world (FranklinCovey, n.d.).

Through the course of his leadership experience, collaboration, and research, Covey has become an authority on trust. He notes that in the business world, trust acts upon two key variables: speed and cost. Between two people, when trust decreases, speed decreases. Due to a low level of trust, time is consumed when one or both parties proceeds with caution, investigates motives, and prepares contingency plans. As a byproduct, cost goes up in equal measure (Covey and Merrill 2018).

According to Covey, trust is built by demonstrating consistent behavior over time. A positive action will not generate lasting trust if it's quickly followed by one that's detrimental to the other person. In this way, he encourages leaders to think about trust like a bank account. You have a separate, unique account with everyone with whom you interact. Your behavior may constitute a deposit or a withdrawal in that joint account. Say a kind word? Deposit. Fail to meet an agreed deadline? Withdrawal. Building trust is about consistently making a series of deposits—even small ones—over a prolonged period.

Many organizations seek to quickly build new products and services, test them, and incorporate learnings from users and customers. They need speed. Consider for example, Emily Mias, a senior product manager at Thrive Global, a behavior change technology company founded and led by none other than Arianna Huffington.

Mias has extensive experience working in fast-paced software startup environments, and she appreciates the critical role of trust. She told me in an interview, "For me, trust is about coming to the table with humility, vulnerability, and a sense of humor." In Covey terms, these are the type of deposits Mias wants to put into others' trust accounts as well as what she wants to see flowing into hers. In an up-tempo startup environment, getting those trust transactions moving quickly is important.

"As a new person who comes on to the team, you can slowly build up your reputation and eventually get to a point where people say, 'Oh, Emily. She's a person.' But I didn't want to do that. A month is my target for when I want people say, 'Oh, Emily. She's a person *I want to go to.* I like her, and she gets things done.'"

In Mias's experience, this type of trust-building happens fastest through one-on-one relationships. She found that building those relationships while working remotely demanded a modified approach. She had to pull a page from her software playbook; she decided to pivot. "During my first week at my new gig, I set up back-to-back one-on-one meetings," she told me. "Those individual relationships are how you learn how to help and build a reputation of being dependable."

"Some people will take longer to warm up to you, of course," Mias says. She explains how in many cases, exploring commonalities beyond the walls of work is helpful. "I like to ask, 'What are you interested in? What do you care about? Oh, do you like dogs? I have a dog here. She's taking a big nap.'" Even once trusting relationships have been established, making it a priority to maintain them is important. The effort pays off.

As Mias puts it, "The more you put yourself out there as someone who's going to fix things or someone who's going to do whatever needs to get done, you start to gain credibility. Later, when you need something or when you see something that needs to be addressed, you'll have the backing you need." For her, this cascade of trust deposits all begins with an attitude of humility and a willingness to be vulnerable.

Jennifer DeHayes echoes Mias when it comes to vulnerability's role in building trust. As a school administrator, DeHayes recognized that to establish a trusting relationship with her teachers, she had to expose herself to a risk of failure and the distinct possibility that her intentions may not come to fruition. When installing a new instructional approach, she said to her teachers, "Look, I'm going to make mistakes. I'm not perfect." By making herself vulnerable, DeHayes built a bridge between herself and each of the teachers she depended on (DeHayes 2019).

Several workplace studies make a strong business case for building trust. Workers in high-trust companies were found to have 75 percent less stress and 50 percent higher productivity than those in low-trust organizations. High-trust workers also had more energy, fewer sick days, higher levels of engagement, and more life satisfaction overall (Zak 2017). High-trust companies were also found to outperform their competitors by 186 percent as compared to low-trust laggards. When embraced by leaders, trust can become a significant competitive differentiator (Ladika 2021).

Expressing commitment is one of the most powerful ways to build trust. I once attended a parent-teacher conference in my daughter's kindergarten classroom. My bride and I took our tiny seats in the back of the classroom while we waited for our turn to speak with the teacher, Mrs. Fairbairn. I looked up at the bulletin board to admire the students' colorful art contributions. That's when I noticed a sign Mrs. Fairbairn had posted for her beloved students.

It read: "I will never give up on you."

Don't our followers deserve a similar level of commitment from us as leaders? Could there be a more substantial foundation for a professional working relationship?

As Covey illustrated, trust accelerates the efforts of any two people pursuing a common goal. Leading others therefore requires building and maintaining trust for results to flow as naturally as possible. This makes trust a sort of lubricant in the machinery of leadership. Without trust, the resulting friction prevents smooth and efficient operations and generates heat in the form of mutual frustration and interpersonal conflict.

FAIRNESS

The Lockheed Martin F-35B Lightning II fighter jet is a trailblazer. Owing to its specific brand of warfighting tactics, the US Marine Corps deploys aircraft that are highly capable in the skies but also have a unique ability to descend vertically into extremely tight parking spots (Lockheed Martin, n.d.). An F-35B pilot can launch from the short runway of a naval vessel, reach altitude, and then accelerate to a speed sufficient to break the sound barrier.

When that pilot is Anneliese Satz, sound isn't the only barrier she's breaking.

Satz became the first female Marine F-35B pilot. To accomplish the feat, she logged more than three hundred flight hours practicing in simulators and completing a grueling series of written and practical application exams. The process took four years of committed effort. She explains, "I truly believe that showing up prepared and working diligently are two major keys to success" (Vella 2019).

Despite being the first female Marine F-35B pilot, Satz explains, "The aviation community has never really been that divisive when it comes to different gender capabilities because a plane is a plane, and it doesn't care who's piloting it." She acknowledges, however, that the same inclusivity has not yet been extended to women in combat roles. "Unfortunately, they've got a long way to go for that" (Spector 2021).

In the civilian workplace, there's an equally long way to go to bridge the chasm between underrepresented groups and those in the dominant culture.

Jodi-Ann Burey is a writer and speaker who has no interest in "business as usual." She observes that in their efforts to create diverse and inclusive work environments, employers often encourage employees to "bring your full selves" to work. This puts an unfair burden on already disadvantaged groups. She explains, "Being authentic privileges those already part of the dominant culture. It is much easier to be who you are when who you are is all around you" (Burey 2020).

The analogy she uses is that of a costume party. Workers from underrepresented groups—those with racial, gender identity, sexual orientation, disability accommodation needs, or other characteristics different from those of the majority—are asked to "come as you are." When they arrive at the party, however, they're surprised and disappointed to find that most of the guests are in full costume, determined to keep up the charade.

Even if a leader is highly attentive to the lived workplace experience of historically underrepresented groups, other forms of potential bias remain.

Personality differences are one often overlooked example. Susan Cain, author of the book *Quiet: The Power of Introverts in a World That Can't Stop Talking*, observes that introverts present complementary strengths and a different style of leadership as compared to their extroverted counterparts. She encourages leaders to be mindful about who around them may be an introvert and what their specific needs are (Insights 2018).

Equitable examples may include providing time for meeting attendees to gather thoughts rather than simply engaging in real-time brainstorming. A leader can also monitor the percentage of airtime to ensure introverts are able to contribute their fair share of insight and expertise.

Neurodiversity is another important consideration when leading others. Tracey Bromley Goodwin and Holly Oberacker are the cofounders of Navigating ADHD, a consultancy that serves children, teens, and working adults. In an interview, Goodwin explained to me, "Everyone's brain works differently. You see how yours works, but that doesn't mean that's the only way or the preferred way." Recognizing that a team member may have an alternative ability or preference when processing information raises your leadership awareness.

Understanding that another person may be having an entirely different experience than others around them is also important. According to Goodwin, "They may be thinking to themselves, 'Why is this email taking me three hours to write when for the person across from me, it only took them ten minutes?' Comparisons like this can lead to internal frustration."

Oberacker shared an example of a client who is impulsive and wildly creative but who has also overwhelmed people with his enthusiasm at times. As a result, he has taken steps to modify his working style. "He's learned to structure his work week to be remote as much as possible because this means less ad hoc interaction with people. He's now able to preserve more energy to think about all the things he's sharing when he does interact."

Drawing back to empathy, acknowledging how others may be feeling is important. Oberacker explains, "A person may feel they have to prove themselves because of a diagnosis they might have, or they may be experiencing imposter syndrome when, in fact, they're the expert in their field. They just don't feel like they are because they're putting so much time, effort, and energy into all of it that others don't see."

Subjecting an employee to an unfair workplace experience is like grounding a fighter jet. Unfortunately, this happens more often than we may care to admit.

In a recent survey, a meager 18 percent of employees felt they are working in a high fairness environment (Gartner 2021). Those employees who consider their work environment to meet perceived standards of fairness boast 26 percent higher performance. They're also 27 percent less likely to quit. Even when a new employment relationship starts off well, it can quickly sour unless it's built on a foundation of fairness. Another study found that a steep decline in organizational commitment occurred among employees who began their work with a high level of trust in management but then experienced unfair processes and outcomes (Seifert et al. 2015).

I smell a rat.

As if the fairness picture couldn't get any worse, we need to return to our helper rats from earlier in the chapter. Remember how good it felt to learn about the helper rats who happily freed their companions and shared their snacks? I'm sorry to report that there's more to the story.

In experiments where the trapped rat is from another, unfamiliar breed, the free rat does not release its cage mate. Neurobiological findings show that the would-be helper's reward system in its tiny little rat brain fails to activate unless the trapped rat is from a familiar breed. In response to this finding, Inbal Ben-Ami Bartal said, "This research shows that the reward system has an important function in helping behavior, and if we want to increase the likelihood of pro-social behavior, we must reinforce a sense of belonging" (Shahar 2021).

In rats, it seems that empathy is conditional. I would like to think that we humans, with our larger brains and an awareness of our special connection with one another, are of a higher order than rats. Yet when I see unconscious bias creep into our leadership—mine included—I have my doubts.

A sense of belonging can certainly enhance empathetic experiences, increase willingness to demonstrate altruism, and even build mutual trust. But rather than demonstrate a preference for interacting with those who are most like us, what if we simply recognized that any notion we're actually separate from one another is the real problem?

CONNECTEDNESS

Carlo Rovelli is an Italian theoretical physicist and the author of *Reality is Not What It Seems: The Journey to Quantum Gravity*. Over the course of 288 mesmerizing pages, he details the conceptual evolution of what we know about the universe and our place in it. He also details how very *little* we know about even the most basic phenomena that constitute our physical reality (Rovelli 2017).

At the microscopic level, at a scale much smaller than even a single atom, things get very weird. Calculations that work in the macroscopic world break down at the quantum level. Scores of physicists have spent decades constructing elaborate experiments and sophisticated machinery to coerce the universe into spilling its deepest secrets. For those of you keeping score at home:

Universe: 1. Physicists: 0.

One of the most fascinating discoveries quantum physicists *have* managed, however, is known as field theory. As Rovelli writes, "particles are quanta of quantum fields; light is formed by quanta of a field; space is nothing more than a field, which is also made of quanta; and time emerges from the processes of this same field. In other words, the world is made entirely from quantum fields" (Rovelli 2017).

To understand this—at least as *I* understand this—imagine that you and I were to visit the beach near my home on Cape Cod, Massachusetts. If we both submerged ourselves under the surface of the Atlantic Ocean, we would each be completely surrounded by water. We would be connected to one another by the waters of the Atlantic Ocean. We would also be connected to the shores of nearby Boston as well as those of more distant Miami, Buenos Aires, Lisbon, and Lagos by the vast and continuous ocean.

Every particle of every—well, *everything*—is similarly suspended in a field that stretches in all directions throughout the entire universe. All physical matter is thus connected. Any appearance of disconnect or discrete physical existence is both relative and conventional. Separateness is, in a word, illusory.

As compared to the miniscule quarks at the quantum scale, a black walnut tree is gargantuan. A mature black walnut tree can reach an astounding height of as much as 120 feet tall. More remarkably, the eventual height and shape of a young black walnut tree is dependent in large part on its neighbors.

In a forest setting, a black walnut that is surrounded by other trees will be straight and tall with only a few lower branches, if any. The connection between the tree and its surroundings determines its growth trajectory; the two are intertwined. This type of connectedness has a dark side, however. The black walnut tree produces a natural herbicide called juglone. Like a mean red triangle, the black walnut tree hinders the progress of nearby plants, thus preserving more resources for itself. I'll leave it to you to determine if that reminds you of any leaders you know.

If the fundamental building blocks of the universe and our ecology are inherently interrelated, does an inescapable connectedness apply to our social bonds as well?

In 1979, a set of identical twins was reunited at age thirty-nine. Having been separated at birth, "the Jim twins"—Jim Springer and Jim Lewis—did not known the other existed (Hayasaki 2018). Researchers in the field of genetic biology often study twins to understand what types of phenomena such as physical health and disease may be the result of our genes versus our environment. Plus, identical twins are just plain fun to look at.

Upon comparing their life stories, the Jim twins were as surprised as the researchers. They were raised by their respective adopted parents a mere forty miles from one another (Sahu and Prasuna 2016). They both suffered from migraines, struggled in spelling and math, and they both bit their nails. As I read this, I thought to myself, "Okay. That's a little surprising, but where's the evidence of a deeper connection?"

Both Jims smoked the same brand of cigarettes. Both drove the same make and color car. Both had worked as part-time deputy sheriffs. Both named their childhood pet dogs "Toy." Their eldest sons were named "James Alan" and "James Allan." Both had married women named Linda. Both had divorced their respective Lindas, and both had remarried women named Betty.

Okay, now you have my attention.

What's truly shocking is that one needn't be an identical twin to experience seemingly unexplained influences coming from the people around them. Nicholas A. Christakis and James H. Fowler are the authors of *Connected: How Your Friends' Friends' Friends Affect Everything You Feel, Think, and Do*. As someone who knows my friends reasonably well yet my friends' friends' friends not at all, I found the authors' premise quite intriguing.

The pair studied human social networks, not in the online sense, but in the form of traditional interpersonal connectedness. Their research produced fascinating findings regarding the connections between varying groups of people as well as what's transmitted over these connections. Their discovery led them to conclude, "How we feel, what we know, whom we marry, whether we fall ill, how much money we make, and whether we vote all depend on the ties that bind us" (Christakis and Fowler 2011, 7).

Much like the earlier example of quantum physics, these connections and their resulting influence upon us often fall beneath our level of perception. The nature of this connectedness, however, is a driving force in what we experience all the same. The authors observe, "In a kind of social chain reaction, we can be deeply affected by events we do not witness that happen to people we do not know."

For us leaders operating somewhere between our quarks and our cosmos, Rovelli was right; reality is not what it seems. At the quantum level, we don't directly see our inherent connectedness, but we can't deny its existence. In our ecology, we don't often think about how all life on earth is entangled. At the level of our social interactions, we don't recognize the invisible influence others have on us. At the level of our consciousness and our collective consciousness, we can barely understand it at all.

Yet in the face of mounting scientific evidence and because of our lived experiences, our connectedness is undeniable. For enlightened leaders, it's any lingering attitude that we are separate from one another that doesn't make any sense.

If you think things got a lot more complicated when we began to Expand the Circle to include one other person, just wait until we invite even more people to the party next.

* * *

TIPS & TAKEAWAYS

1. **Make the shift.** Move beyond your self-interest by concerning yourself deeply with others' experiences, objectives, strengths, limitations, and circumstances. Put their welfare and success on par with your own.

2. **Feel the feels.** Exercise your empathy muscles by pausing to consider what those around you may be feeling. You are specifically wired to take on others' perspectives, so don't tamp down this powerful human ability.

3. **Act accordingly.** Push past any reservations and take steps to improve the well-being and circumstances of others. You may not directly experience a corresponding

benefit in the short term, but leadership is about the long game.

4. **Do the math.** Remember that trust increases speed and reduces effort. Extend trust early and willingly by making yourself trustworthy and invest in building and maintaining trust in your relationships with others.

5. **Level it out.** Enlightened leadership is about equanimity and exchange. Seek equity in your relationships with others, not by pretending that you have no biases but rather by being aware of them and offsetting them to your best ability.

6. **Connect the dots.** Increase your awareness and appreciation regarding how we're all intrinsically connected in ways we don't always consider. Tap into our unique human bond to boost the flow of positive intent and action between us.

LEAD YOUR TEAM

Sticks in a bundle are unbreakable.

—*KENYAN PROVERB*

For as long as I can remember, team-based work has always landed me in a peculiar position: on the ground. As a Little League second baseman, I delighted in diving for ground balls. As a grade school basketball point guard, I lunged to steal the ball from an opposing player. As a Marine radio operator, I gathered intel, "stood" watch, and slept, all while on the ground.

Despite the vertically challenged nature of these team experiences, I loved them all. The camaraderie of a high performing and enjoyable team experience is simply unrivaled. Team dynamics can be hard to influence, but when we get them right, they have a mystical, memorable quality all their own.

When we Expand the Circle beyond pairs of relationships, we reach the level of our Team. At the team level, group dynamics are more complex and fluid; environmental and social factors can threaten the team's performance, welfare, and commitment. An enlightened leadership approach allows us to tilt the odds in our favor. We can draw our teams closer to us, achieve our target outcomes, and ensure the growth and well-being of our team members along the way.

VISION

On a fateful day in 1940, Thomas Hull's car broke down just south of Las Vegas. While waiting for roadside assistance, he noticed something peculiar; a significant percentage of the license plates that whizzed by were *not* from Nevada (Horridge 2017). The predominant highway that shot diagonally from Los Angeles to Salt Lake City and back had seen a huge surge in traffic. Hull was already the owner of two motels in California, and at that moment, he decided that his next project would be located on that dusty stretch of desert highway. This new hotel, however, would include a casino.

Hull's proposal went over worse than a pair of eights at a blackjack table.

He found a plot of fifty seven acres for the hotel-casino complex he had already constructed in his mind. The woman who owned the arid acreage considered it to be worthless, but she accepted his check for $57,000 anyway. Developers inside the Las Vegas city limits considered his idea to construct El Rancho Vegas on its outskirts to be "insane" (Al 2020).

Hull was unphased. To make his vision a reality, he knew he needed to assemble a capable team. He tapped his longtime architect, Wayne McAllister. He hired ten gardeners decked out as cowboys to match El Rancho's motif. The band wore

Western-themed outfits, too, as did the "El Rancho Starlets," a troupe of showgirls who hailed from Hollywood. The team constructed the first resort-casino complex on what would later become the famed Vegas Strip.

It all began with Hull's ability to see what nobody else had. Whether you're disrupting an entire industry or commanding a small team, you must develop and communicate a vision for collective success.

One of the most powerful questions a leader can ask is "What's possible?" An active imagination allows us to peer into the future, whether that be a week, a quarter, a year, or multiple years, depending on our responsibilities and level in the organization. We can forecast future market conditions, risks, and opportunities.

One aspect of imagination is even more distinctly human, however. Imagination lets us take on others' perspectives so that we might "experience the world differently" and "have the capacity to connect in meaningful ways" with those around us (Judson 2021). For example, Hull imagined that travelers driving through the desert would be desperate for refreshment and a respite from the relentless heat and sun (Hopkins 1999). That's why the El Rancho didn't shield its swimming pool from view like other properties; it proudly put its pool on display next to the highway. This led the *Saturday Evening Post* to proclaim, "It was a stroke of showmanship. No traveler can miss the pool; few can resist it" (Al 2020).

The seeds of innovation take root in an imaginative mind: one that has been primed by experience. This happened for

Janet Echelman, an artist and sculptor. Early in her career, she studied calligraphy in Hong Kong and textile arts in Bali (Zeiger 2016). While preparing for an art exhibit in India, Echelman needed inspiration. She said, "I went for a walk on the beach, watching the fishermen bundle their nets into mounds on the sand. I'd seen it every day, but this time I saw it differently—a new approach to sculpture." Her power of imagination allowed her to utilize the lightweight fishing nets to create novel forms. Today, her massive, undulating installations perform colorful dances high above slack-jawed spectators at sites all over the world.

These dramatic and highly visible examples aren't the sole domains of imagination's impact. In large ways and small, leadership directions, decisions, problem solving, and actions all stem from the wellspring of imagination (Judson 2021). Any new product, service, operating method, or mechanism in your organization was once the figment of a leader's imagination.

Now that your right brain has had a workout, it's time to get your left brain in on the vision game.

Critical thinking can be defined as "careful goal-directed thinking" (Hitchcock 2018). If imagination answers the "What's possible?" question with its head in the clouds, critical thinking does so with its feet firmly on the ground. To be successful, leaders must strike a balance between creativity and feasibility.

A leader may need to engage in several critical thinking activities, for example, when developing a new course of action.

This may include becoming well informed about relevant issues, defining terms and context, and defending a position or viewpoint (Ennis 1993). The same leader may employ a related set of critical thinking activities while engaged with their team members. The leader may also need to evaluate the credibility of sources or metrics these team members cite, test assumptions they make in their argument, and ask them clarifying questions.

For these reasons, employers have long cited critical thinking as a highly desirable skill among job seekers (SHRM 2019). Fortunately, critical thinking is a skill leaders and employees can develop through deliberate study and practice. Leaders can also guide teams to progressively higher levels of critical thinking abilities by helping team members execute, synthesize, recommend, and generate plans of action (Plummer 2021).

In developing the concept for El Rancho Vegas, Hull struck a proper balance between creativity and feasibility. His experience as an entrepreneur helped him answer the "What's possible?" question using both sides of his brain. He made a novel connection between location and opportunity, *and* he had the market sizing, revenue, and cost projections to defend his dream.

All that was left was to impart his vision to his team in a way that garnered their enthusiasm and commitment. In short, he had to tell them a story.

In my own leadership, I've put a great deal of effort into the art and science of storytelling. When I was an inexperienced leader, I leaned too heavily on my analytical abilities.

I expected my rationale to speak for itself. During a meeting, I would be excited to see heads nodding. After a week or so passed—sometimes after an hour passed—I was disappointed when any forward momentum fizzled.

I soon discovered that I was failing to make a critical connection.

Nancy Duarte is a writer, speaker, and CEO. She's a communications expert whose Silicon Valley consulting firm has helped develop tens of thousands of presentations. According to Duarte, "Stories are the most powerful delivery tool for information—more powerful and enduring than any other art form" (Duarte, n.d.).

I invested time learning storytelling fundamentals and techniques from experts like Duarte. I studied Joseph Campbell's *The Hero with a Thousand Faces* and his recognition of "the hero's journey" in stories throughout human history. I consumed Carmine Gallo's *Talk Like TED* to glean storytelling secrets from the best presenters. More importantly, I diligently incorporated these techniques into my communication. I improved, and I became a more effective leader as a result.

Much of a leader's work involves some degree of organizational change. Here, Duarte again highlights the importance of storytelling saying, "Stories have the power to convey transformation" (Duarte and Sanchez 2016, 15). Leaders often find themselves amid something known as information asymmetry; they have it, and others need it. As Duarte describes it, "As the story's communicator, the narrator typically knows what others can't or won't understand and uses that insight to illuminate everything" (Duarte and Sanchez 2016, 15).

Hull's insight from the roadside just outside Las Vegas created a desert transformation that proved to be illuminating indeed.

When NASA compiled a series of photographs taken from space as part of its "Cities at Night" collection, it made special note of the Vegas Strip (Evans and Stefanov 2008). Widely regarded as the brightest spot on earth, the Strip glows with the concentrated energy of millions of neon lights from massive resort-casinos that followed Hull's lead. Hotel magnates bought into Hull's vision and flocked to the Vegas Strip to be a part of it.

IDENTITY
Harvey Catchings played eleven seasons in the National Basketball Association. While Catchings never became a superstar, his entry in the NBA history books holds the distinction of being super weird. The final box score for the November 8, 1978, matchup between the New Jersey Nets and the Philadelphia 76ers indicates that Catchings played fourteen minutes for the Nets (Nets, n.d.).

He also played two minutes for the 76ers in that *same game.*

During the third quarter, an overzealous official issued a flurry of technical fouls which led to the ejections of Bernard King, the Nets' star player, and Kevin Loughery, the

Nets' coach. When the Nets later protested the outcome, the league office concurred and ordered that the end of the game be replayed at a later date. By the time the teams met again to finish the game, Catchings and several other players had been traded between the two teams. When the game officially ended more than a month after it began, three players had effectively switched sides.

The switcheroo may have been amusing to historians, but it was jarring for the players. Catchings said, "That's when it really hit me, when I walked on the court and saw all of my old teammates. I thought no way would they let us do this, but then you see the clock and the guys you spent four and a half years with now on the other side, it was mind blowing" (Powell 2018).

Once we identify as part of a team, letting go can be hard.

In my experience, team identification is a powerful yet under-utilized tool in the average leader's toolbox. Team morale and performance can both benefit when team members incorporate identity with the group into their own identity. One study found that team effectiveness increased in line with team identification. This led the researchers to conclude that team identity "unites individuals around team goals" (Reis and Puente-Palacios 2019).

There appears to be a bidirectional relationship between team identification and team dynamics, in fact. Team identification has been associated with lower levels of conflict regarding both task completion and relationships among team members. Therefore, relationships are a popular category for employee engagement survey questions; they increase the likelihood of team identification.

Many of the interpersonal dynamics we learned about in the prior chapter are present in the team context as well. For example, trust and fairness are foundational elements in a proper leadership relationship between two parties. At the group level, these characteristics are similar in nature, but they impact the team dynamic in a much more complex way.

In a recent study, researchers found that a leader's ability to create and foster a team environment perceived as fair by its members can enhance team members' feelings of inclusion. This sentiment also contributes to the adoption of a positive team identity even when conflict or differences of opinion arise (Ellemers et al. 2011).

Trust also reappears in the team context. Where team identity was found to be positively related to team effectiveness, the relationship was mediated by the level of trust team members had in one another and with the team leader. Considering how slow trust can be to develop and how difficult it is to regain trust when lost, researchers concluded that "it is essential for employees to actively cultivate the trust of their organizational members both in management and in one another" (Han and Harms 2010, 35).

Long before Catchings shot a jump shot for two different teams, we find that some form of group identity dates to the earliest tribal and clan cultures of human history.

Fast forward to modern times, however, and the nature of team-based work and team identity is much more complex. Teams in the modern workforce are often separated by distance, made up of highly diverse individuals, dependent upon a bevy of digital communication methods, and experience rapidly shifting membership (Haas and Mortensen 2016). On a given day, a typical knowledge worker may find themselves working as a part of several teams. It would be like an NBA player also being part of a football team, a rugby team, and a baseball team all at the same time and while exclusively connected to other team members by Zoom.

If team identification was overlooked by leaders before, it's nearly invisible now.

As an effective team leader, you must find a way to encourage team identification. It's critical to create a shared mindset among the members of your team. This can be done through sharing information to foster collective understanding and by nurturing a cohesive team identity (Haas and Mortensen 2016). This is the essence of "we" thinking over "me" thinking.

I've had the great honor of coaching and training teams of varying shape, size, and seniority. When working with a new team, I begin by asking the team leader "What's your team's name?" Shakespeare might disapprove. He wrote, "What's in a name? That which we call a rose by any other name would smell just as sweet." Perhaps, but to be fair, Juliet never had to deliver a sales quota or conduct a code review. I've found that among sales teams and agile software development teams, the name game is strong.

Jim Speredelozzi is a sales executive who has led revenue-producing teams in high growth software companies for more than twenty years. Speredelozzi told me, "Team names create a sense of community and connectedness. Teams with names are more motivated by their sense of purpose. It's the same reason we like the 'Red Sox' more than the 'Boston Baseball Players Team.'" This matches my experience when leading software product professionals, as well. They partnered with agile software developers and user experience designers to collaboratively name their scrum teams.

Examples of sales team names—replete with sales lingo—include *The Cash Cows*, *Peaches and CRM*, and *Who's the Boss?* (Moorehead 2021). Not to be outdone, agile software team names include equally creative monikers such as *Scrum and Coke* and *Bit by Bit* (Scrum, n.d.). Whether a team name is clever or not, its ability to increase team identification is what's important.

Would you feel a sense of community or belonging if you were part of the hyper-descriptive *"accounting department"* team or worse yet, *"We're responsible for rolling out the new employee handbook"*? If your team only has a hierarchical or functional name—or doesn't have a name at all—it makes it hard to incorporate the team's identity into your own sense of self.

Team identification isn't enough to create a high-performing team, however. Even if a team enjoys a strong sense of team identity, sooner or later somebody on the team is going to be asked to defer their own needs for the greater good.

COOPERATION

On a nature reserve in Myanmar, a long table sat in a field. A tray of bananas rested at each end of the table. A group of nine semi-wild Asian elephants slowly paced about, studying their predicament. A short wall stood between them and the delicious banana bounty. They studied a length of rope that extended through a hole in the wall, through a pair of fittings attached to the table and back through another hole in the wall.

Whenever an elephant pulled on one of the protruding rope ends, it slipped through the fittings. After a few tries, however, the elephants discovered that if two of them each pulled on an end of the rope at the same time, they could slide the table toward the wall and close enough for their trunks to reach the trays of bananas. Researchers carefully observed these pachyderm partners, noting that members of the group successfully cooperated more than 80 percent of the time across nearly 1,800 trials (Li et al. 2021).

Cooperation is highly dependent on how well teams collectively communicate, collaborate to solve problems, make decisions, and execute. A team is more than just a group of members who pursue their respective individual goals alongside one another. A true team requires cooperation among its members to produce a desirable collective outcome. A leader's role, therefore, is not simply to aggregate the efforts of team members but rather to integrate their collective efforts to produce results that enrich the entire group.

In organizations, the environment in which teams operate tends to be quite complex. A given team may experience situations involving limited resources, competing goals, or stylistic differences among team members. Some teams must endure all of these at the same time. Teams also may have dynamic membership or task assignments. Under these circumstances, cooperation can become challenged at best. Whatever the context, leaders can increase the likelihood of team cooperation by fostering commitment, collaboration, and compromise.

Commitment relates to the team's dedication to being a member of the team as well as to its collective aim. Research has shown that team commitment relates to servant leadership behaviors such as those presented in the earlier chapter (Mahembe and Engelbrecht 2013). When servant leadership increased, so did the overall effectiveness of the team. This effect was moderated by the team's commitment level, however. Only high levels of servant leadership *and* team commitment produced the highest levels of team effectiveness.

Another study explored the relationship between commitment, trust, and teamwork behaviors. Both trust and teamwork behaviors influenced the overall commitment levels of team members (Sheng, Tian and Chen 1970). Similarly, higher levels of teamwork behaviors positively influenced trust. As a leader, reinforcing these aspects of the team dynamic has a similar interconnected, beneficial effect to that of other social factors we've seen earlier.

Organizational work presents a seemingly endless array of problems to solve. Teams have significant advantages over individuals when it comes to problem solving, as collaborative teams are better able to pool resources, exchange ideas and information, and combine the perspectives of diverse team members. Each team member may bring their own unique expertise or analytical skill set to the problem-solving effort. A team leader can boost collaboration by modeling collaborative behaviors themselves and by balancing task-orientation and relationship-orientation (Gratton and Erickson 2007).

Another characteristic of successful teams is a willingness to compromise when necessary. This happens whenever a team member must sacrifice their own individual interests in deference to the collective aim of the team. In some cases, a team member may need to defer their individual goal attainment for a period while the team's attention and resources are directed toward those of another team member. Or a team member may need to take a supporting role instead of a driving role to create a more effective team configuration overall.

When I was leading a product team, one of my team members preferred a working style that was much different than mine. I'm a fast thinker and an even faster talker. I like to develop and process my ideas aloud, and I've never met a whiteboard undeserving of my furious scribbles as I devise my latest master plan. I was fortunate to have a project manager named Blanka van Raalte who handled all my team's translation needs. Unlike me, van Raalte is steady, thoughtful, reserved, and precise.

One day, I let loose a fury of ideas about how we could approach a new project. I could see the horror in her eyes. She prided herself on performing her job well, and my shoot-from-the-hip style was preventing her from doing so. At that moment, she and I came to an agreement; I would slow down and clarify exactly what I needed, and she would become more comfortable with a wee bit of ambiguity. I suggested that I could muster enough discipline to document a sticky note capturing my success criteria and recommended actions.

In an interview, van Raalte later shared her perspective on our new arrangement. "I was excited to try something new and at the prospect of having clear success criteria when executing a project." My natural style clearly hadn't been working for her, and as a leader, it was up to me to find a workable compromise for us.

She continued, "Our new approach allowed us to have a conversation without me having to capture everything you were saying in the moment. Now, we both had something we agreed on, and I could refer to it to guide my work." The improvements weren't restricted to our process and outcomes. "When the project was over, seeing that sticky note brought a smile to my face and reminded me how my manager considered my working style when leading me."

Over time, I learned to bend my leadership style to meet the needs of my team members. I was able to use my perspective and experience to help them negotiate better working relationships, as well. It wasn't always easy, and it wasn't always perfect, but cooperation helped us boost our team performance and our collective experience.

Having said that, I'm afraid it's time to discuss the elephant in the nature reserve.

Remember our banana-loving cooperators? After two elephants pulled on their respective ends of the rope, the table drew near, and they each gained access to a tray of bananas. I can imagine them low-fiving one another in celebration. The researchers decided to up the stakes, however. Rather than two trays of bananas, they wondered what would happen if they only placed *one* tray of bananas on the table. Would the elephants continue to cooperate in the face of scarcity?

I'm sad to report that cooperation among the elephants quickly fell to zero (Li et al. 2021). While the bananas could have been divided among the cooperators, they opted for more competitive behaviors including mitigation strategies such as "block," "fight back," "leave," and "submission." These bad behaviors are eerily similar to a few I've witnessed—and even perpetrated on occasion—in team settings far removed from a nature reserve in Myanmar. Even if your team has unlimited access to bananas, you're likely to experience scarcity in the form of a lack of role clarity, available resources, leader and peer attention, praise, and recognition.

As a leader, you must work to integrate your team members' efforts and interests. You can increase the likelihood of cooperation by increasing team commitment, collaboration, and—when needed—compromise. The balance is delicate, but things get much easier when you encourage team members to buy into the team's identity, goals, and values.

SAFETY
During a tense boardroom meeting, a group of executives were discussing the competition. One of the executives urged the group to acknowledge their competitor's considerable capabilities. Another highlighted the technical merits of

their own product, downplaying the competitive threat. A third, more senior leader countered that while the product's strength was formidable, it was not unassailable. When the product-centric executive pushed back, the senior leader choked him nearly to the point of unconsciousness.

At least that's how the scene played out in *Star Wars: A New Hope* (Lucas 1977).

Your organization may not be an evil empire intent to use its Death Star to destroy a rebel alliance, but overly aggressive and hostile group dynamics can destroy teamwork in any organizational setting. Somewhat surprisingly, the opposite set of behaviors is equally counterproductive.

Amy Edmondson is a Harvard Business School professor, a researcher, and an author. She once told a story of a manufacturing company in the Midwest whose senior leaders were trying to design a new strategy for the firm (Grant 2021). Rather than speak up, challenge assumptions, or raise pertinent issues, the leaders tiptoed around any potential disagreement. Favoring vagaries and circular dialogue, the group was reluctant to engage on the topics that mattered most, and the conversation went nowhere.

The culprit in both troubled team situations is a lack of psychological safety. According to Edmondson, "Psychological safety is a climate in which one feels one can be candid. It's a place where interpersonal risks feel doable—interpersonal risks like speaking up with questions and concerns and half-baked ideas and even mistakes" (Grant 2021). In a team setting, these behaviors are essential to problem solving, planning, innovation, and other highly desirable organizational activities.

In her book, *The Fearless Organization: Creating Psychological Safety in the Workplace for Learning, Innovation, and Growth*, Edmondson explains that while safety encourages team members to speak up, this is just the beginning. She shares, "The true test is how leaders respond when people actually do speak up. Stage setting and inviting participation indeed build psychological safety, but if a boss responds with anger or disdain as soon as someone steps forward to speak up about a problem, the safety will quickly evaporate" (Edmondson 2019).

Leaders are presented with a particularly difficult choice when a high performer creates a lack of safety among the team.

Marcel Schwantes is an author and leadership coach. In an interview, Schwantes presented me the question he poses to leaders who are facing this dilemma: "What's more important here? A culture of psychological safety or keeping rock stars happy?"

In deference to the high performer's contribution, the leader may downplay their bad behavior. Schwantes explains this by saying, "There's a fear element in which leaders are afraid to lose their star performer because doing so might reflect on their own performance as leaders." Tolerating bad behavior by any team member speaks more about the leader's *real* values than any poster in the breakroom or cringey corporate coffee mug.

Schwantes encourages leaders to take actions to instill and preserve a sense of psychological safety. This includes creating a bond with employees, keeping them informed about developments that affect them, and addressing any issues face-to-face (Schwantes 2022). These actions convey empathy and commitment to team members' welfare and the team's mission. They affirm that the employee matters every bit as much as the results they produce.

Psychological safety sits precariously at the intersection of the team dynamic and team performance.

For example, in one study, Edmondson found that a perception of safety increased the likelihood that errors were reported and therefore learned from in a healthcare setting (Edmondson 2004). An environment of safety has a positive impact on the team dynamic as well. Enhancing safety can lead to improvements in team members' relationships and openness with one another (Jha 2019). Safety has also been found to be the byproduct of an authentic leadership style and a contributing factor toward workplace engagement (Maximo, Stander and Coxen 2019).

Taken together, these create a flywheel effect. Using techniques from our earlier chapter on leading oneself, authentic leadership can contribute to creating an environment of safety, which can improve team performance, which can strengthen team commitment. These daisy-chained outcomes can create even higher levels of team engagement and performance. The leader's job is to build momentum by establishing an environment of safety and then keeping that momentum going by preventing setbacks or addressing threats to maintaining it.

Psychological safety is also inherently required for another leadership capacity we've discussed in a prior chapter: fairness. As Edmondson describes it, "As we go from diversity to inclusion to belonging, psychological safety is needed more and more at each level for this to be the case. It's hard for me to imagine feeling a sense of belonging in a place where I didn't feel I could bring my full self to that place" (Grant 2021). Like fairness, safety is built by trust and destroyed by fear.

Which brings us back to a galaxy far, far away.

It turns out that toxic bosses like Darth Vader may not be *all* bad. At least they show us how not to behave. In a study of supervillains in film, graduate student Jens Kjeldgaard-Christiansen observed that "all bad guys are incredibly antisocial and try to control all resources with no regard for anyone but themselves" (Griffiths 2016). This is the antithesis of the type of safety and prosocial leadership behaviors that are the hallmark of this book and related leadership theories. Unfortunately, most readers will have had a run in with a toxic boss or team member at some point in your career. While uncomfortable to experience, observing these malicious behaviors may create an aversion to displaying similar shortcomings in your own leadership.

COHESIVENESS

Imagine that you're taking a walk through a meadow on a crisp, cool spring morning. The sky is big and bright. You're surrounded by lush green grass and a colorful blanket of wildflowers. The air is damp and fragrant. You notice a spider's web nearby, and you lean in to take a closer look. Hundreds of dew drops decorate the web. Some drops are large, and some are small.

But *how* are they there at all? Why don't the dangling drops simply trickle down into the soil below?

Cohesion is a physical property whereby molecules of the same type tend to stick to one another. In the case of a dew drop, the force that causes the water molecules to stick together and to the web is stronger than the force of gravity.

In the context of working teams, cohesiveness is defined as "that group property which is inferred from the number and strength of mutual positive attitudes among the members of a group" (Summers, Coffelt and Horton 1988). This is essentially the degree of attraction members feel toward one another and toward membership in the group. A cohesive team is one where we feel a strong sense of connection to one another. We enjoy being around one another as much as we enjoy doing our collective work. This definition seems relatable to any team player.

Unfortunately, it's a bit more complicated than that.

It turns out that cohesiveness presents an unusual challenge in the field of organizational psychology. In a paper titled *Defining Group Cohesiveness: A Legacy of Confusion?* the author notes that "group cohesiveness has proven to be astonishingly difficult to define precisely and consistently"

(Mudrack 1989). Another article states, "Group cohesion is difficult to measure; the lack of a precise and rigorous definition of cohesion contributes to the difficulties of measuring the construct" (Summers, Coffelt and Horton 1988).

Yet even if psychology nerds can't define cohesiveness in their terms, we've all felt it. We've all felt its absence, too. This phenomenon speaks to the art of leadership rather than purely to its science. The discipline of leadership is a human endeavor; it can't strictly be reduced to ones and zeros or purely objective constructs and measures.

Sometimes, leadership is a leap of faith.

When I was driving to the office one day, I was involved in a minor car accident. Another driver struck the rear passenger door of my car before speeding away. I was frustrated but uninjured, so I continued to the office.

When I told my three product team members why I was late for our morning meeting, they were very supportive. Bill said he had a friend who worked in a junkyard. Rick said he had a toolbox in his trunk. Allen joked that we should visit the junkyard as a type of team building exercise.

Only I didn't laugh; I led.

We piled into my bruised car, and we made a morning of it. We replaced the damaged door with one that *almost* matched the original. We howled when we realized that the interior was a different color, and the exterior had a nifty pinstripe that the rest of the car lacked. Afterward, I treated my team to a victory lunch to celebrate our mechanical prowess.

In the months that followed, our work environment became more challenging. The pace of product development demands outstripped our engineering capacity. Sales targets escalated quickly as did the pressure to exceed them. Some teams lost good people. Despite the challenging circumstances, our product team became stronger than ever.

The cohesive properties of water create a phenomenon known as surface tension. This happens when the topmost water molecules that cannot bond with the air bond even more strongly to one another. That's exactly what happened to us; we clung more tightly to one another as the situation worsened. As a result of this experience and countless others like it, I don't need an objective, academic definition of cohesiveness. I know that cohesion is real, and it's spectacular. It boosts team performance, and it's worth developing.

Creating cohesiveness is the high art of effective team leadership. You can create the same type of tight bonds that hold your employees together like those glistening dew drops that form under the morning sun. Team performance and experience will increase. When you get it right, you'll transform your team and yourself in the process.

At that point, you'll be ready to think even bigger.

* * *

TIPS & TAKEAWAYS

1. **Get it together.** Recognize that a team can accomplish exponentially more than isolated individuals. Create conditions for team success by applying enlightened leadership principles at the collective level.

2. **Tell me a story.** Clarify your objective to create energy and momentum. Hone your ability to craft compelling stories and make a habit of sharing them with your team to keep them moving in the right direction.

3. **Play the name game.** Humans are wired with a need to belong. Foster a tangible identity for your team and ensure that team members see the inherent benefits in group membership and the collective pursuit of the team objectives.

4. **All together now.** Enhance collaboration and mutual sacrifice in pursuit of team objectives and the overall welfare of team members. Be mindful that competing goals and competing styles are natural byproducts of team-based work.

5. **Safety first.** Create an environment where team members are unafraid of the repercussions of membership, offering a counterpoint, or highlighting risks and challenges. Psychological safety is a prerequisite to effective teamwork.

6. **Make it stick.** Difficult times can either pull your team apart or bring it together. Strengthen the bonds between team members through recognition, appreciation, and honesty to create an enduring connection.

LEAD YOUR
ORGANIZATION

Only three things happen naturally in organizations: friction, confusion, and underperformance. Everything else requires leadership.

—*PETER DRUCKER*

The USS Inchon was an amphibious assault ship commissioned in 1970. This "gator freighter" was my seafaring home for six months, which included a deployment to the Red Sea as part of Operation Continue Hope. The US Navy ship was essentially a floating city. Its technical infrastructure—from ballast to boilers to bulkheads—was complemented by its human infrastructure. More than 1,400 sailors and wobbly-legged marines worked in unison to keep the Inchon functional, safe, and relatively comfortable.

The ship's captain played an important and high-profile role, but any single leader can only do so much. It took a complex mesh of teamwork to keep the Inchon humming. Cross-functional teams performed maintenance duties, operated the flight deck, and provided health services. Even the barber shop churned out an endless supply of buzz cuts as a team.

No hierarchical chart with layers of jobs and dizzying reporting lines could fully depict how the Inchon *actually* worked. When we arrived off the coast of Mogadishu, Somalia, the Inchon's crew and its Marine guests sprang into action. We launched helicopters from its flight deck and waves of hovercraft—one of which included yours truly—from its massive belly. Over one thousand service members executed orders as a dynamic yet cohesive whole.

When we Expand the Circle beyond a single team, we reach the level of the Organization. Drucker's quote above suggests that organizations have a default tendency to produce undesirable consequences. This is what happens when we allow organizational dynamics to depersonalize our work and rob us of our human nature. By taking an enlightened leadership approach, however, we can unfetter our organizations' potential by properly channeling the impact and vitality inherent within them.

MISSION

The world's fastest train belongs to the Central Japan Railway Company. The Lo Series Maglev train is a sleek speedster which glides above its tracks using magnetic levitation technology. Once the prototype becomes fully operational, it's expected to trim the time required to cover the 300-plus mile distance between Tokyo to Nagoya from two hours and thirty minutes down to a crisp one hour and seven minutes (Carrick 2021).

Magnetic levitation technology uses two sets of magnets. One set repels the train up and away from the tracks, and a second set pulls the train forward. These twin magnets minimize friction, facilitate a high rate of speed, and create stability. In an organizational context, we look for similar results in the form of efficiency, agility, and brand loyalty. Before we can produce these desirable outcomes, however, we must first articulate our mission to employees and customers alike. Anything less creates the type of friction that can grind a train—or an organization—to a screeching halt.

An organization's mission shapes the products and services it offers, its goals and objectives, and its operating philosophy. Some missions are ambitious and inspiring, while others are more pragmatic. Without a clearly defined mission, core organizational activities lack important context. This creates a tremendous amount of friction that can slow down or even stall important internal functions like decision making and communication. Companies that lack a clear and compelling mission may also inadvertently create brand confusion or erode customer loyalty among external stakeholders.

Like twin magnets, a worthy mission lifts employees up and away from internal day-to-day friction and draws customers and other external stakeholders forward toward satisfaction and long-term affiliation. Both forces are essential to an organization's growth and prosperity.

There's ample evidence supporting the relationship between an organization's ability to cultivate a sense of purpose through its mission and its resulting business performance. Across more than fifty years of research spanning a variety of industries and business strategies, a positive relationship has emerged time and again (Cardona and Rey 2022). Another study found a positive relationship between how coherent and readable an organization's mission statement is and its resulting financial performance (Cortés-Sánchez and Rivera 2019). Pursuing a mission you can't understand is difficult.

Mission statements seem to guide important organizational activities beyond the numbers, as well. In an analysis of mission statements, researchers made two important discoveries (Bartkus and Glassman 2008). First, relatively few mission statements include references to social issues such as the environment and diversity. More reassuring is the second finding that those that did were also more likely to demonstrate organizational behaviors supporting the cited issues. By contrast, generic references to stakeholder groups—think employees, customers, community—were more common, but specific activities to support these groups were less likely to be pursued beyond the statements themselves.

Considering mission's central role, it seems as if every leadership team would craft a tidy mission statement to share with employees and the outside world. Unfortunately, doing so isn't as easy as we might think. Complex dynamics are involved in every organizational setting. To assuage a diverse array of needs and stakeholders, many mission statements become so watered down or so vague they barely say anything at all.

Customers, shareholders, and employees may have competing interests, and satisfying any set of needs often involves making tradeoffs (Hooper and Pye 2002). For example, a leadership team may consider investing in an employee development program, but doing so would reduce the return to shareholders. Building a new facility to support future growth may impinge upon natural resources at the construction site. How can leaders find a North Star to guide their organization-level initiatives as they navigate these tradeoffs?

Simon Sinek is the celebrated author of *Start with Why: How Great Leaders Inspire Everyone to Take Action*. Sinek created a simple but powerful management framework consisting of three concentric circles (Sinek 2009). The outermost circle is labeled as WHAT a given organization, product, or service does. The middle circle describes HOW it does this. The innermost WHY circle is the essential mission, intention, or purpose driving the endeavor.

Many executives, marketers, and product managers obsess over their WHAT. Enamored with the details, they seize every opportunity to call attention to these highly tangible elements of value. Sinek, however, urges leaders to work from the inside out by spending more time and energy clearly understanding and articulating their WHY.

Leaders who find their WHY reduce friction that otherwise causes employee confusion and wasted energy. By clearly articulating their WHY, they create a powerful attractive force that compels the organization forward. Employees and customers directly experience benefits at the individual level, as well. Sinek (2009, 95-96) writes, "When people inside the company know WHY they come to work, people outside the company are vastly more likely to understand WHY the company is special."

Kelly Breslin Wright is a technology executive who personally experienced the attraction of an effective mission statement. Prior to joining Tableau, a data visualization company, she was inspired by the company's mission which states, "We help people see and understand data" (Gong.io 2021). This pithy phrase was more than a mere marketing tagline. It captured the essence of the company's WHY. It helped the company recruit top talent like Wright, prioritize product investments, and win and serve customers. The clarity of its mission is part of the reason Tableau grew faster than a bullet train. The company was founded in 2003 and was acquired for $15.7 billion in 2019.

If you're a level-down leader, you may not have input on writing your organization's mission statement, but you have two important roles to play all the same. First, you should see your organization's well-crafted mission statement as a type of guidebook to guide your prioritization and decision making activities. Second, you have an opportunity to help others see themselves in the mission in order to embrace their higher sense of purpose.

Magnetic trains reach alarming speeds by dramatically reducing common sources of friction. Enlightened leadership is similar in its aim. Clearly articulating a compelling mission produces a similarly smooth result in an organization. Like a pair of magnets, the mission stabilizes the operation for employees and accelerates value for external stakeholders.

CULTURE

In 1941, George de Mestral went for a walk in the woods. Once his walk ended, he became intrigued by the cockleburs that clung to his dog's fur. De Mestral was a Swiss engineer, and his curiosity led him to examine a cocklebur under a microscope. Under magnification he saw that each cocklebur had hundreds of miniscule hooks, each poised to snag on a bit of fabric or fur. He spent the next ten years developing an extremely versatile fastening system. His eureka moment became the birth of VELCRO®, a trademark he created by combining the French words for velour (velvet) and crochet (hook).

Inside our organizations, we can think of VELCRO® as an apt analogy for culture and cultural fit. Our policies, ceremonies, practices, decisions, and actions are like loops in the company's culture. Prospective and current employees come along cocklebur-style with their personal values outstretched like tiny little hooks. If an organization has a strong culture, it can snag workers who are a natural fit and keep them hooked in place. A weak culture, by contrast, produces flimsy bonds at best.

Julie Ann Sullivan is a business culture expert and the author of *Catalysts of Culture: How Visionary Leaders Activate the Employee Experience*. According to Sullivan, "Your culture defines your company, your brand, your customer loyalty— it is fundamental to everything that you do" (Glazer 2020). Culture plays such an important role that she refers to it as "the fabric of a business."

Despite its critical role, not all cultures are created equal.

When working with leadership teams, I teach that three types of culture exist: inadvertent, inauthentic, and intentional. I call the first type inadvertent because many organizations allow their cultures to emerge without any real forethought. These ad hoc cultures are created when executives and employees hold unspoken beliefs and simply act in ways that feel most natural.

The second type is the most nefarious of the three. An inauthentic culture is one where an organization lists a gleaming set of values on its careers page and on posters in its breakrooms, but it fails to act in accordance with these. Candidates are duped into accepting a job offer only to learn the hard truth too late; employees who do stick it out quickly become frustrated and distrusting of the organization.

An intentional culture gets the gold star. It's not the result of chance but instead comes from deliberate design, both top-down and bottom-up. Creating it and maintaining it is the responsibility of the most senior leader as well as leaders at every level.

The CEO or business owner arguably has the strongest influence on the company culture. In a study, researchers looked at the relationship between the personal values held by a CEO and the corresponding organizational culture (Berson, Oreg and Dvir 2008). They found that CEOs having self-directed personal values tended to lead innovation-oriented organizations. Similarly, those senior executives having security or benevolence values were more likely to lead organizations with bureaucratic or supportive cultures, respectively.

Even if you don't have a CEO title, you're a leader, and you have a role to play in shaping organizational culture. Hema Crockett is a culture expert and the author of *Designing*

Exceptional Organizational Cultures: How to Develop Companies where Employees Thrive. In an interview, Crockett pointed out that while the culture of a company may begin by mirroring that of its founder, "As the company starts to grow and more people come in, we start to really see that culture is recreated." An organization's culture is continually reshaped by its decisions, actions, rewards and punishments, and the preferences of its new hires.

This phenomenon reflects the critical role leaders at every level play in deliberately influencing and protecting the organization's culture. Crockett notes that this happens whether we're conscious of it or not. "A lot of times as leaders, we don't realize how much we're being watched. Our team and those around us are taking their cues from what we're doing." Our attitudes and behaviors send not-so-subtle signals as to which values, attitudes, and behaviors are desirable and which are less important or counterproductive.

When a leader believes a culture needs retooling, this may be an opportunity for pruning rather than planting more seeds. Patty McCord is a human resources consultant and the former chief talent officer of the entertainment superstar Netflix. In her book *Powerful: Building a Culture of Freedom and Responsibility,* McCord (2017) asserted that the culture at Netflix "wasn't built by developing an elaborate new system to manage people" but instead by "stripping away policies and procedures." She advises leaders to begin with the mission and then to work backward to examine each current system and ask whether it accomplishes the objective or not (Ramsey Network 2018).

She cited an example where Netflix made a dramatic change to its paid time off policy; they eliminated it. Rather than strictly regulate holidays and time off, the company offered its employees the autonomy, flexibility, and responsibility to choose for themselves when to take leave. The result? Employees took the same amount of time off, but they felt more empowered by being given the autonomy of being able to choose for themselves. This led McCord to conclude that "giving people ownership and trust is so much more effective than a policy" (Creating 2018).

Strong evidence suggests culture influences the performance of an organization. Corporate cultures have been found to influence employee performance and employee satisfaction (Ahmad 2020). These benefits impact the short- and long-term horizons of employee welfare. In the larger sense of the organization, culture guides the formulation of new strategies (Byles, Aupperle and Arogyaswamy 1991). At the individual level, culture offers an employee a much-needed collective identity and social support.

Based on her experience at Netflix, McCord captured the cocklebur-like clinging power of culture by saying: "True and abiding happiness in work comes from being deeply engaged in solving a problem with talented people you know are also deeply engaged in solving it" (McCord 2017).

Whether viewed through the lens of problem or purpose, a distinctive culture will snare the right cocklebur candidates and employees. Once this type of intentional culture and social fabric are in place, leaders at every level must constantly reinforce it so it sticks.

ALIGNMENT

The spring morning is beautiful. The sun is shining, and the warm temperature has coaxed an endless variety of creatures from their slumber. A buzz permeates the air, both figuratively and literally. A beekeeper approaches the colony situated in her backyard. Inside the colony, there is one queen, hundreds of male drones, and tens of thousands of female worker bees.

For millions of years, bees have engineered complex social organizations. They've developed incredible means of communication and coordination. Each bee knows its job role, and each is integrated in a collective pursuit of the survival of the queen and the health and well-being of the colony. Somewhat surprisingly, they do this without the benefit of one-on-one meetings, Zoom web conferencing, or data-driven dashboards. The delicious honey the bees produce is a byproduct of their high levels of orchestration and execution.

Alignment has been defined as "a shared understanding of interdependent systems, practices, and routines of the organization (Alagaraja and Shuck 2015). Organizations are complex; as such, alignment is difficult to establish and even more difficult to preserve. When misalignment happens, it causes all sorts of problems including squandered resources, missed opportunities, and an escalation in costs that can besmirch the bottom line. The human toll is arguably worse since misalignment drains individuals' energy stores, increases disengagement, and boosts the likelihood of turnover.

Owing to their massive size, scope, and scale of operations, large enterprises are all the more susceptible to misalignment.

For more than a century, enterprises have turned to an array of management techniques such as spans of control, matrix organization structures, and synchronized top-to-bottom cascades of objectives. Today, organizations are awash in a real-time stream of electronic communications and access to minute details and metrics regarding the operation of the business.

Despite all this, true alignment remains as elusive as ever.

In an organizational context, success is a collective endeavor. Leadership inside an organization, therefore, is about mobilizing all the resources of the entire enterprise despite their constant motion and interconnected nature (Trevor 2018). In their book *Alignment: Using the Balanced Scorecard to Create Corporate Synergies*, management theorists Robert S. Kaplan and David P. Norton note that higher performing enterprises are "better at aligning their corporate, business unit, and support unit strategies" (Kaplan and Norton 2006). This reflects the interaction—and cooperation—required between centralized and decentralized groups.

Even so, leaders at smaller organizations shouldn't regard misalignment as the exclusive domain of mega-corporations. Misalignment can derail a company of any size. Consider a growing software company with one hundred employees. The senior leadership team cannot personally meet with each employee in a given month, much less every day. How can they make sure everyone is maintaining a shared understanding of the company's mission and values as well as its operating systems and routines? When done right, this is where alignment emerges as a significant competitive advantage.

Like a hive, an organization exists precisely because its collective structure provides an advantage over the loose marketplace. Consider that very few activities in the average organization cannot be offered by freelancers or contractors. The effectiveness and efficiency of being able to organize employees to do this work is part of what Kaplan and Norton refer to as "enterprise-derived value" (Kaplan and Norton 2006). The pair observe that "for a corporation to add value to its collection of business units and shared-service units, it must align these operating and service units to create synergy."

When thinking about our organizations and workers, the whole is greater than the sum of its parts, and misalignment threatens both performance and employee experience.

Maribel Olvera is a technology executive with a background in operations management. She has a unique vantage point from which she observes an organization's strategy, alignment, and the effect the presence or absence of alignment can have on employee performance and welfare. In an interview, Olvera told me, "If people at any level of an organization are not clear as to what their contribution is, they're just showing up for the money, and nobody wants to show up just for the money." She notes that employees want to know they're having an impact on something bigger than themselves. They want to see they're making progress and moving some needle in a way that matters.

Olvera came to appreciate alignment down to the employee level in part by analyzing employee engagement survey results. "Whenever we had teams that were clear in their contribution toward our mission, their engagement levels were higher." When developing leaders in her organization, she encourages them to spend time with each employee to help them see how they are contributing to the macro goals.

She also insists that they choose measures and outcomes that are in the direct control or influence of the employee. For example, giving a customer satisfaction target to a customer support team is too broad. Reducing time to resolve problems is getting warmer. Providing customer sentiment to the product team in a way they can easily absorb is highly actionable for a customer support team. In one instance, by taking corrective action at the level of individual alignment, Olvera saw the employee's engagement level—and energy— increase as a result.

Something about our work and the technical way we approach it unnaturally distances us from the organization's social fabric. In many cases, a leader may find that it's beneficial to encourage employees to reinsert a social prerogative. Jeff Kavanaugh is the author of *The Live Enterprise: Create a Continuously Evolving and Learning Organization*. He likens organizations to a dynamic, organic system—one where its individual constituents see themselves as enmeshed in a social whole (Kavanaugh and Tarafdar 2021).

Kavanaugh shares that it's possible to help every employee understand, "You've got the ability to serve someone else . . . you're helping them improve their lot in life" (Taylor 2021). By highlighting that one's efforts have immediate beneficiaries, boosting belonging and impact at the same time is possible. Kavanaugh refers to this as a type of "enlightened self-interest." I want to know that the work I'm doing matters, and I want to see how it's serving those around me.

What we're seeing unfold is how alignment is both a phenomenon and a practice that exists at the macro and the micro levels. Leadership techniques, therefore, should also be applied at both those levels depending on the position of a given leader.

In his book, *Measure What Matters: How Google, Bono, and the Gates Foundation Rock the World with OKRs*, the accomplished Silicon Valley investor John Doerr (2018) describes an empirical alignment framework involving Objectives and Key Results (OKRs). This systematic approach to linking an organization's WHY and its HOW creates top-down alignment in the macro sense. Doerr (2018, 10) also highlights the micro impact of misalignment on the individual when he writes, "When people have conflicting priorities or unclear, meaningless, or arbitrarily shifting goals, they become frustrated, cynical, and demotivated."

Tempting as it may be, placing too much emphasis on the mechanics of a business is a misstep. While we spend gobs of time talking about our metrics and outcomes as well as the processes and procedures that produce them, we do so at the risk of missing the bigger point. Alignment is essential for employee productivity and employee welfare. Employees need to experience "psychological agreement between individual and organizational goals" (Alagaraja and Shuck 2015). A lack of such congruence leads to a series of maladies.

At this point, buzzing back to our friends the bees is helpful.

The hive is analogous to an organization. It is highly complex and exists within the context of shifting dynamics such as food supplies, membership, weather, and external threats. It is simultaneously a social enterprise. Each bee performs its work and contributes in some way to one another and to the health and welfare of its neighbors and the entire hive. Alignment means that at any given moment, the bee is both part of the hive's execution *and* the experience it is providing. In human organizations, alignment represents the harmonization of the needs of the work to be done with those of the workers doing that work.

WELLNESS

How many portable devices do you use daily? From our phones to our wireless headphones to our e-book readers, our modern conveniences are never far from us. The utility of these glorious gadgets depends in large part on their rechargeable batteries. French physicist Gaston Planté invented the first rechargeable battery in 1859 (Brain, Bryant and Pumphrey 2021). More than 150 years later, the dreaded "Low Battery" warning sends us scrambling for the nearest outlet.

In the workplace, employees aren't fueled by literal batteries, but they need ample opportunities to recharge all the same. They expend their energy in pursuit of our organizational objectives. As the beneficiaries of their efforts, we leaders have a responsibility to help them recharge and restore their levels of well-being.

Employee well-being has three primary characteristics (Wright and Huang 2012). First, it's subjective. Employees must *believe* they are well to be considered well. Second, it's emotional. Well-being includes physical well-being but also an affective dimension of how they are experiencing positive and negative emotions. Third, well-being is a holistic phenomenon involving the employee's aggregate life including their life beyond the workplace.

Awareness and interest in workplace well-being has recently increased. Much of this interest stems from the strong relationship between well-being and organizational performance.

"The case for well-being at work is indisputable," says Laura Putnam, author of *Workplace Wellness that Works: 10 Steps to Infuse Well-Being and Vitality into Any Organization* (Liu 2022). She goes on to say, "Give me any metric that matters to your organization, and I'll show you how it ties to well-being: productivity, profitability, innovation, employee engagement, talent retention, customer service, safety, you name it."

For our part as leaders, we need to take accountability for the environment that we're creating for our employees. To gain this perspective, Putnam says, "My advice to leaders is to stop and consider whether the people in their organization are healthier, happier, and more enabled to be the best version of themselves because of where they work—or less so."

Interest in HR-provided employee wellness programs has exploded. The success of these programs requires several key characteristics including the use of multiple communication channels to maximize awareness and making services accessible and convenient (Mattke et al. 2013). Wellness should be seen as a priority and a critical success factor by leaders at every level and not just within HR and People Operations. Organizations should also take full advantage of existing resources like those related to healthcare benefits that may be underutilized. Finally, organizations must continually monitor program effectiveness and associated results and remain aware of the shifting wellness needs of the workforce.

A comprehensive answer to whether the organization is making employees healthier isn't just about centralized wellness programs, however. Individual awareness and intervention are also needed. Organizational issues like chronic stress, peak workloads, and a toxic work environment can have disastrous effects on employee well-being.

Chris Dyer is an acclaimed speaker and author. In an interview, he shared a series of practical tips he provides leaders to help address and increase employee wellness. For example, he observed that with the advent of remote and hybrid work formats for knowledge workers, we've lost a clear delineation for when we're at work and when we're not at work. If a college grad both sleeps and works in her bedroom, she's lost an important environmental cue. Therefore, Dyer encourages leaders to "help people create signposts" that will allow an employee to "have a clear start and stop." Otherwise, there's a risk of a constantly draining battery.

Dyer shared another pair of creative techniques revolving around our omnipresent meetings, whether they take place in the room or on the Zoom. He recommends beginning a meeting with the question, "How is everyone showing up?" While the common question "How is everyone?" tends to produce a superficial stream of "Fine"s and "Okay"s, "How are you showing up?" triggers a deeper and more personal response and connection among the meeting members.

At the end of the meeting, Dyer asks, "How is everyone leaving the meeting?" This question is a check-in regarding the technical bits—the meeting's outcomes—as these reactions and perceptions shape the environment and its subsequent downstream impact on employee well-being. If a team member is frustrated that they didn't get the decision they wanted, the leader should surface this and be prepared for its lingering effects.

With so much attention currently being paid to office perks and centralized programs, some leaders may be tempted to think that wellness is the responsibility of the HR department. This is more than a major missed opportunity; it's a reckless attitude that can harm an employee's experience and their intent to stay. Who better than an employee's direct manager to individualize the response and coaching the employee needs to experience a heightened sense of wellness?

Organizations that prioritize employee wellness reap a multitude of benefits. One example study found that increased well-being was associated with improved job performance and presenteeism (Hamar et al. 2015). Another team of researchers noted that over the past two decades, "Research has consistently found a significant well-being to job performance relationship" and that "the importance of well-being in the prediction of employee retention has long been recognized" (Wright and Huang 2012, 1189).

In yet another study, individuals who were made to feel happier had an approximately 12 percent increase in productivity (Oswald, Proto and Sgroi 2015). Organizations that don't prioritize employee wellness are more likely to experience a productivity drain due to employee lapses in physical and emotional health, challenges at work, and issues at home.

Like a rechargeable battery, centralized programs and individual interventions have the potential to restore energy in the form of employee well-being. Work is demanding, and energy flows naturally from the individual into the work we hire them to do. As senior leaders, we need to ensure that we're making a top-down investment by providing access to programs and systems that promote employee wellness. At the individual level, frontline leaders need to actively check in with employees to raise our awareness—and theirs—regarding current levels of wellness and ways we can work together to improve long term health and happiness.

BENEVOLENCE

After positioning the final log in its resting place, an eager beaver dredges up mud armful by stubby armful to seal the dam. What was once a gently flowing stream now features a beaver pond. The beaver next turns its attention to building a dome-shaped lodge with an underwater entrance to ward off would-be predators.

The beaver isn't the sole beneficiary of its labor, however. The pond it created produces a hospitable habitat and a food source for several other fish and wildlife species (Beaver Solutions, n.d.). Beaver ponds support thriving salmon populations and may even benefit humans by reducing erosion and risk of flooding (National Geographic, n.d.). Beavers are considered a *keystone species*; they create and support entire ecosystems through the output of their industrious efforts.

The same could be said of enlightened organizations.

The Cambridge English Dictionary defines benevolence as the quality of being kind and helpful. In our organizations, this relates to the downstream benefits that flow from how we conduct our business. Groups ranging from boards of directors to frontline employees to consumers have increasingly emphasized what's known as the "triple bottom line" of profits, people, and planet. The resulting question is both direct and far-reaching: How is the world a better place with your organization in it?

Leaders are now called upon to set their sights higher than business performance alone. They must also pay dividends in the form of Corporate Social Responsibility (CSR) and sustainability efforts. Shareholders who once demanded sky high profits above all have gradually morphed into stakeholders who keep score in a radically new way.

Sustainable business strategist Andrew Winston (2021) observes that "companies are increasingly expected to play a positive role in society and take responsibility for the broader effects of their actions and products." Lynn Sharp Paine, author of *Value Shift: Why Companies Must Merge Social and Financial Imperatives to Achieve Superior Performance* agrees, noting that "the superior performers of the future will be those that can satisfy both the social and financial expectations of their constituencies" (Paine 2003, xi).

Like a beaver lodge, a business can be a mechanism to serve its owner's needs as well as those of a far-reaching set of stakeholders. Considering the self-absorbed track record of most business, however, reason for skepticism remains. Some way to transparently prove good intent and measure outcomes is needed.

In 2007, organizations began to embrace a new mechanism to accomplish these aims. A certifying body known as B Corp emerged to create and advance an exacting set of standards. B Corp certification allows an organization to "build trust with consumers, communities, and suppliers; attract and retain employees; and draw mission-aligned investors" (B Lab, n.d.). More than 4,000 companies representing more than 150 industries have earned B Corp certification.

While the direction is positive, the results of the effort have been mixed. A team of researchers conducted an intensive review of the available literature studying qualitative and quantitative B Corp performance. In terms of productivity, they concluded that "the conclusions are diverse and, on some occasions, contrary." (Diez-Busto, Sanchez-Ruiz and Fernandez-Laviada 2021, 2508). In fairness, measuring new achievements with an old ruler is difficult. If a given B Corp were massively profitable, one would have to question whether it wouldn't have been possible to do *more* to benefit its stakeholders. We have only just begun to keep this new set of books.

If relying solely on our heads is proving too limited for this new frontier of business, perhaps we will do better if we turn to our hearts.

In their book *Conscious Capitalism: Liberating the Heroic Spirit of Business*, John Mackey (cofounder of Whole Foods Market) and Rajendra Sisodia (distinguished professor at Babson College) describe nothing less than a highly evolved economic system (Mackey and Sisodia 2014). "To be conscious means to be fully awake and mindful, to see reality more clearly, and to more fully understand all the consequences—short term and long term—of our actions," the pair write.

When we wipe the lenses that have clouded our view of a corporation's purpose for thousands of years, we come to a stark realization. Mackey and Sisodia (2014, 275) note, "A business that generates financial wealth but destroys other forms of wealth (which can have greater impacts on people's well-being) adds far less value to the world than it is capable of."

The pair make a strong case that shifting to a more conscious form of capitalism isn't just nice to have; it's quickly becoming a matter of competitive differentiation and survival. We've already seen that the latest generation of consumers are intent to spend their money with companies they trust; they will quickly turn their backs on brands they feel are bad actors.

While conscious, heart-centered governance would have been tantamount to treason in the boardroom only a few decades ago, there is a growing sense that we must press even further.

What if the new world of work is pulling us further from our moorings, beyond the head and beyond the heart?

Alan Murray is the CEO of Fortune Media. In his book *Tomorrow's Capitalist: My Search for the Soul of Business*, Murray notes that the development of a more benevolent form of business is "the result of far-reaching changes in the world that were demanding a new social compact between business and society" (Murray and Whitney 2022). We've long seen the soul show up in our *Chicken Soup* self-help titles, but not in a tome from one of our largest business press leaders. A change is definitely in the air.

Hubert Joly captures the unsettling nature of first becoming aware of this profound shift. While working as a McKinsey consultant, he heard the CEO of a massive global enterprise observe that an organization's true purpose lies beyond its profits. Joly later reflected, "This went against everything I had learned in business school and over my early career as a management consultant" (Joly 2021).

His later experiences as the CEO of Best Buy during its turnaround as well as more recent conversations with other like-minded executives led him to observe, "Companies are not soulless entities. They are human organizations made of individuals who work together toward a common purpose."

Thinking of human organizations in terms of our human existential evolution isn't a stretch. Recall how Maslow's hierarchy of needs culminated in self-transcendence. If the pinnacle of human experience is an abandonment of ego and an absorption in the interest of others, will the same not be true of our organizations in the future?

Enlightened leaders at every level have an opportunity to shape that future. If you're an executive, you can reorient your organization's purpose to deliver results to the new triple bottom line. Level-down leaders, you can reinforce the benevolent aspects of your organization's mission, ensuring that it resonates with those nearby. You can create critical connections between your team members and their opportunity to serve a broader set of stakeholders through their day-to-day work.

As a keystone species, beavers serve countless others while going about their work. Organizations and leaders have a similar opportunity to architect an arrangement that will permit benevolence to flow freely to downstream stakeholders. More than just a thoughtful notion, this enlightened leadership approach is quickly becoming an expected means of operation and the basis of competitive advantage.

* * *

TIPS & TAKEAWAYS

1. **Get moving.** An organization is like a freight train. It takes a great deal of energy to get it started, and its momentum can make it difficult to maneuver. Stay vigilant at the controls.

2. **Lock it in.** Be intentional when defining and supporting your mission and purpose. Its magnetic qualities will keep you on track and propel you forward.

3. **Stick together.** With culture, consistency and reinforcement are key. Communicate your culture broadly and take steps to ensure attitudes and behaviors constantly reflect it.

4. **Act as one.** You can only achieve a multiplier effect from aligned efforts. Be mindful of the competing goals and splintered interests that naturally crop up in complex situations.

5. **Get well soon.** By making employee wellness a priority, you care for those who make everything possible. Their health and happiness will show up in the workplace and beyond it.

6. **Broaden your reach.** Include the full range of stakeholders when assessing your impact. Benevolence is a responsibility, an opportunity, and a wise investment in holistic success.

LEAD THE WORLD

The wide world is all about you; you can fence yourselves in, but you cannot forever fence it out.

— J. R. R. TOLKIEN

One of my favorite activities growing up was visiting the Gateway Arch in Saint Louis, Missouri. The stainless-steel arch curves high above the ground topping out at 630 feet. Its crisp, smooth lines glisten under the Midwest sun. The world's tallest arch features a tram system that can ferry forty passengers to the top in around nine minutes each way. As my family boarded a tram, I bounced in my seat with excitement.

Once we reached the viewing platform, I sprung out of the tram car. I leaned against the walls to peer out a series of small windows. On a clear day, seeing thirty miles into the distance is possible. While the other spectators stared horizontally out toward the surrounding landscape, I fixed my gaze straight downward.

From this unique perspective, the people meandering around the mall at the base of the arch indeed looked like ants. What struck me most, however, was how my perception of them— and myself—suddenly shifted. They certainly weren't thinking about me, but I was thinking about them. I delighted in this type of detached sense of self. For whatever reason, being separated by elevation, steel, and glass didn't cause me to feel isolated from them at all. I could *see* them, and for that reason I felt a profound connection with these strangers who I would never meet.

Just when it feels as if we can't Expand the Circle any further, we discover that we can pass beyond the boundaries of our organizations out into the World. Many of the circumstances outside our organizations are concerning, and a dearth of leadership is perpetuating the challenges we face. An enlightened leadership approach, therefore, aims to extend the benefits earned in the earlier layers so we may have a positive impact on a limitless set of stakeholders. Removing artificial barriers between us and the world allows our leadership to flow to where it's needed most: everywhere.

FAMILY

The front door swings open, and an exhausted parent slams the door behind her. She trudges into the living room, shoulders slumped, before crumpling on the couch in a heap. Her young son looks up from his homework and quips, "Tough day at work?" Cue the laugh track.

TV sitcoms have portrayed family dynamics for decades. They often juxtapose characters' family lives against their work lives. Mike Brady of *The Brady Bunch* was an architect. Animated dad Homer Simpson worked at a nuclear power plant. On *Blackish*, TV mom Rainbow was an anesthesiologist. A view of family life without work is incomplete whether it plays out on a Hollywood sound stage or wherever you call home.

Considering the pace and pressure of the modern work environment, avoiding taking our work home with us in some fashion is nearly impossible. Working parents can find themselves particularly strapped. In one study, nearly a third of parents working from home reported having at least some child-care responsibilities that compete for their attention and effort (Danley 2021). For these employees, daily life is a whirr as they vacillate between the demands of the office and the household.

The advice often given to employees with families is as elusive as it is obvious: "Seek balance." Yet when there's not enough time, attention, or energy to fully satisfy all the demands, employee health is depleted. Overtaxed workers may become physically and mentally exhausted, irritated, emotionally distanced from their children, or inadequate or ineffective in their relationships (Brennan 2021). These health consequences can create a downward spiral that's increasingly difficult to escape.

Employers play an important role in creating a working environment that helps employees perform at their best at work *and* at home. The United Nations Children's Fund urges employers to be flexible by offering the option to work from home and allowing employees to modify their working hours around their family demands as needed (UNICEF, n.d.). They also encourage granting new mothers sufficient maternity leave and offering parental training to workers in need.

Hilton is a company that has been recognized as being exceptionally family friendly. For example, the hotel giant partnered with Thrive Global and Stanford Medicine to create the Parenthood Journey Program (DiversityInc 2019). The program offers training for leaders with employees who are new parents as well as video education for moms on topics such as connection and well-being. Family-centric initiatives like this contributed to Hilton's being recognized as the #1 Best Workplace for Parents by *Fortune* magazine (Stories from Hilton 2019).

The relationship between work and family dynamics doesn't flow in only one direction. In fact, your family experience may have shaped your work experience even before you began your professional life. A *Harvard Business Review* article describes how early family experiences can shape our expectations and interactions in adult life including our world of work. Its author, Roger Jones, noted that, "Early family life affects how leaders respond to pressure and react when team members compete for their attention" (Jones 2016). In a nod toward boosting self-awareness, he encourages leaders to examine their earliest family experiences to look for significant events or recurring beliefs and values.

In a classic TV sitcom move, you can also flip the script.

Many of the lessons and experiences you glean from the working world are directly applicable to your family life. The

US Department of Health and Human Services suggests that leading by example, demonstrating effective listening and communication skills, and being able to motivate others are all ways to exercise everyday leadership skills in the family context (Tips 2019). The same is true with the insights and practices we covered as we expanded earlier circles ranging from self-awareness to trust to cooperation to benevolence and everything in between.

In his book, *The 3 Big Questions for a Frantic Family: A Leadership Fable… About Restoring Sanity to The Most Important Organization in Your Life*, Patrick Lencioni asks a very curious question: What would happen if we were to manage our families as if they were businesses? (Lencioni 2008). After framing the answer through the lens of a fictitious family, Lencioni delves into familiar management techniques such as clarifying values, defining measurement systems, and reporting out status. This shouldn't be altogether surprising. I know many working parents whose kitchen whiteboards forecast their kids' whereabouts better than Logan International Airport's flight control. Why shouldn't we borrow things that work when we're *at* work to make our family lives more manageable?

I did exactly that when my kids were younger. My Saturday morning "family meetings" became notorious. My bride and our three kids would issue an audible groan as I beckoned them to the living room for my latest installment. I would read my prepared instructions aloud before diving into meeting time. I did my best to keep the time requirement brief, the energy high, and the lesson crisp. If you've spent any amount of time in the working world, you will find my meeting content eerily familiar.

In one meeting, I created a March Madness–inspired bracket that pitted personal values in head-to-head matchups. After a few minutes of easy then more difficult tradeoffs, each family member read their results from the Championship Round aloud. I was shocked and amazed by their diverse choices! We all delighted in learning about one another and about the role values play in our lives because of this simple exercise.

During another family meeting, we each took turns navigating a blindfolded family member toward an objective to learn about trust and communication. In another, we saw how high we could each adhere a sticky note to a tree. Then we learned just how much higher we were able to reach when we worked together by standing on one another's shoulders.

Years later, we were sitting around a firepit reminiscing about the kids' bygone youth. When the subject of our family meetings came up, I was impressed at how vividly they recalled those experiences. Despite the occasional eye roll, they thoroughly enjoyed my efforts to bring my leadership home. By breaking down a wall, I created a critical connection.

Just like a one-sided sitcom script, work-life compartmentalization doesn't paint the full picture. Remote work, ubiquitous screens, and flex time have further comingled these two domains beyond separation. Everyone needs to recognize when one, the other, or both need a time out. An enlightened leader doesn't fall for the delusion that you can do it all or that you can strike a perfect balance. Instead, enlightened leadership is about seizing the opportunity to bring these worlds closer together.

Wins at work can spill over to our home lives and vice versa when we recognize the intrinsic connection between everything that occupies and surrounds us. Our efforts to artificially divide ourselves reduce our capacity, while efforts toward integration amplify our energy, enthusiasm, and results.

When we push past the boundary of work and bring enlightened leadership to our family context, we do more than set the example. We reverse the downward spiral and allow ourselves to be fully present for those who mean the most to us.

COMMUNITY

Monowi, Nebraska, is situated on the Cornhusker State's northeastern border with South Dakota. Like most other small towns in rural America, most days are quiet there—exceptionally quiet, in fact. Monowi has no schools, no stores, and no stoplights. When it comes to residents, the town doesn't even have people; it has a *person*, singular. The 2010 census listed Monowi as having "Population: 1," that one being a woman named Elsie Eiler (Murphy 2011).

Eiler is the owner of Monowi Tavern at the center of town. She's also the town's mayor, so she issues herself a liquor license and pays herself taxes each year (Francome, Garner and Stein 2020). Practically speaking, Eiler *is* the town. The United States encompasses approximately 19,500 incorporated towns and places. In these communities, residents may have less influence over their operation and welfare than Eiler has on hers, but they have a similar opportunity to make an impact through their everyday leadership.

Communities aren't restricted to governments and geographies; they include any group of people sharing common characteristics and interests. Military veterans and their spouses, for example, make up a very large and dedicated community. Unfortunately, being a part of this particular community comes with unique challenges. Long separations due to overseas deployments, a constant threat of violent conflict, and frequent moves are just some of the realities facing military families.

The unemployment rate among military spouses has hovered between 24 percent and 30 percent for the past decade (Hiring Our Heroes 2022). The constant moves, the day-to-day responsibilities of military life, and an inability to access affordable childcare are all barriers to employment for spouses, 92 percent of whom are women (Opel 2021).

As a Marine Corps officer's wife, Michelle Penczak struggled to secure a job. After dozens of interviews, she began working as a virtual assistant (Colosi 2019). She excelled in her work. When one of her clients asked her to scale up, she committed to do so but only if she were able to join forces with other military spouses. Today, she serves as the CEO of Squared Away, the virtual assistant company she cofounded. The company's mission is to employ as many military spouses as possible, currently more than 300 and growing (Mortensen 2020).

In an interview, I asked Penczak why she had been so committed to creating a workforce comprised of military spouses like herself. "They were my friends," she said. "I had been working in a virtual capacity for so long, and I had girlfriends who were asking me, 'How the heck can you move from North Carolina to Hawaii and still have a career? How do I get into that?'" She felt deeply connected to her community, and she took steps to align their respective interests.

Today, Squared Away clients are just as committed to supporting the community. As Penczak puts it, "Military spouses are kind of the underdogs that never get talked about. Clients enjoy being able to support military families, especially since we're a company of all females right now. Our clients tell me, 'This is so amazing. We just want to be able to support you as much as possible.'"

Through her leadership, Penczak was able to not only build a successful business but also one that extended beyond its own interests to benefit her community. In this enlightened arrangement, the positive contributions between leader, organization, and community flow freely in all directions.

Amazing things happen when organizations build bridges between their businesses and the communities they serve.

Founded in 1976, Habitat for Humanity works in local communities in every US state and approximately seventy countries (About, n.d.). The nonprofit focuses on creating adequate and affordable housing for community members in need of support. Each year, tens of thousands of volunteers work together on a variety of housing and construction projects. From demolition to framing to finish work, teams of organizers and volunteers provide the handiwork and reap the rewards of their combined labor.

Corporate partnerships are essential to helping Habitat fulfill its mission. Many partnering organizations afford their employees paid time off to work on projects in their local communities. Doing so makes good business sense. Individuals and teams who work on projects experience higher levels of morale and are more likely to remain with their organizations (Corporate Giving, n.d.).

One example of a longstanding Habitat for Humanity corporate partner is the appliance manufacturer Whirlpool. The company has been a partner for more than twenty years and donates equipment and expertise in addition to volunteer hours. Whirlpool employees are partnering on projects in Europe, Africa, Latin America, and the Asia-Pacific region (Corporate and Foundation, n.d.). The homes they build provide much-needed shelter but also an enhanced sense of gratitude and self-worth on the part of the grateful occupants. The organization is building homes and building communities in the process.

When we bring enlightened leadership into our communities, we reinforce critical connections. We are a part of our communities, and they are a part of us. We can bring the best of our leadership outside of our workplaces and into our communities for their benefit and for ours in return.

For some, this type of enlightened exchange can be life changing.

Sarah Bond-Yancey once attempted suicide. Fortunately, she found meaning in her life through volunteerism. According to Bond-Yancey, volunteering "means stepping outside of your own set of often all-consuming personal issues and refocusing on what is truly important in life: family, community, shared humanity" (Habitat Advocate, n.d.) By directly supporting community members through Habitat for Humanity, she gained a fresh perspective on what matters most. She made a critical connection. Volunteering is not about helping others as much as it's about experiencing how profoundly interconnected we are. She now realizes that "all human liberation and well-being is bound up together—families beside volunteers and advocates beside donors. It fosters the critical partnership between those who need allies and those who need greater purpose, greater depth."

You can expand your leadership to benefit members of your community in many ways. A quick web search on Volunteer-Match.org instantly revealed volunteer opportunities in my community related to gardening, spending time supporting hospice residents and their families, and being a blood drive donor ambassador. Schools, community centers, and healthcare facilities often need the help and support of thoughtful volunteers.

Even if you're short on time, you can always be thoughtful and kind in your interactions with others as you tick off your to-do list across town. Each interaction with another community member is a leadership opportunity. Whether you're having your tires rotated, paying for groceries, or picking up your dry cleaning, each transaction involves an exchange with a fellow human being. Enlightened leadership means taking advantage of the opportunity to brighten someone's mood, inquire about how their day is going, or make a connection if only for a moment. If all else fails, wish them well and be grateful for their assistance.

On the fiftieth anniversary of Monowi Tavern, Elsie Eiler had company. On that Friday afternoon, dozens of people visited the tavern to share their appreciation for Eiler (Knapp 2021). Well-wishers included law enforcement officials who Eiler counts as regulars along with farmers from the extended vicinity. Eiler's grandson even flew in from the Netherlands to be a part of the celebration. Our communities vary in size, circumstance, and characteristics, yet all are deserving of our service within them. We must be willing to pour our leadership into our communities to the benefit of their members and ourselves.

SOCIETY

The first Nobel Prizes were awarded in 1901. Named for the Swedish chemist and inventor Alfred Nobel, the prizes recognize the highest achievement in chemistry, medicine, physics, literature, and peace (NobelPrize.org, n.d.). Nobel decided that after he passed, his considerable fortune should be "annually distributed in the form of prizes to those who, during the preceding year, shall have conferred the greatest benefit on mankind."

This was quite an unexpected gesture for someone a French newspaper once labeled "the merchant of death."

Nobel's vast wealth resulted from his invention of dynamite and a variety of weapons. While he claimed to be a pacifist and that his interest in explosives came from the theoretical chemistry challenges they posed, he profited tremendously from his patents and the production of war armaments. He felt his work was justified, writing that "on the day that two army corps can mutually annihilate each other in a second, all civilized nations will surely recoil with horror and disband their troops" (Tägil 1998).

Not exactly.

Nobel's enterprise was entangled with human suffering and, in his mind at least, human welfare. The byproducts of our organizations and our own efforts as leaders are similarly intertwined. Some organizations and entire industries impinge human welfare. Their profits endanger our health, welfare, and happiness. Others are neutral in their impact. Others have a net positive effect on humankind. Every leader and organization falls somewhere along this spectrum.

Some organizations have reached the highly desirable state where they've figured out how to do well by doing *good*.

Considering human accomplishments and progress, extreme poverty is a blight on our societal record. More than 700 million people live on less than $2 a day, and a third of people in urban areas live in unsafe or unhealthy slums (Lifewater International 2020). When we pause long enough to look at what's happening beyond the boundaries of our organizations and our day-to-day working lives, we often see unsettling things.

In 1986, Jacqueline Novogratz became disenchanted with her work on Wall Street. She shifted her industrious efforts half a world away, cofounding the first microfinance institution in prewar Rwanda. She later wrote about her experience and her mission in her book *The Blue Sweater: Bridging the Gap Between Rich and Poor in an Interconnected World*. Novogratz's perspective shifted as she came to fully realize the true nature of connectedness and its elusiveness. She later wrote, "We are connected, but the weave is sometimes fragile" (Novogratz 2010). Her experiences and her compassion lit the path of enlightened leadership, and she acted.

Novogratz founded Acumen, a socially oriented investment firm, in 2001. Acumen has since invested more than $135 million in social enterprises (Acumen, n.d.). Acumen is not a charity, however. Through its efforts, the firm is building and growing businesses and producing returns with poverty reduction as its chief aim. During a talk, Novogratz (2010) observed that, "very small investments can release enormous, infinite potential that exists in all of us." Her enlightened leadership extends well past Acumen's boundaries by contributing to society in a much broader sense.

Year Up is another organization whose reach stretches beyond its traditional borders. It aims to bridge the divide that prevents many under-served young adults from getting the education, skills, and opportunities they need to succeed in the professional world (Year Up, n.d.). Year Up provides mentorship and training programs for young adults and places them in internships offered by corporate partners. Many of these under-served individuals are blocked from opportunities due to their background, income, or zip code.

The partnering organizations and employees who participate in Year Up programs often benefit as much as the young people they serve. Charkie Quarcoo witnessed these positive experiences firsthand when she served as an associate director of partner relations at Year Up. As Quarcoo told me in an interview, executives were drawn to Year Up's mission and the opportunity to make a positive social impact, but they also felt that the partnership opened a pipeline of talent to which they otherwise wouldn't have had access. This is another example of being able to do well while doing good.

Partnerships required more than executive-level sponsorship, however. "It wasn't good enough just to have a C-level person say, 'Yes, we should do this.'" Quarcoo shared. "We had to get buy-in at every level because we wanted to make sure that the managers really were invested." In this way, all leaders in an organization had the opportunity to connect themselves and their team members to the society-enhancing mission and something bigger than themselves. Their acts of service helped leaders raise and answer important questions. Quarcoo provided several examples. "What does it mean to be a servant leader and to be a leader within my organization? What do I want my career arc to be? What do I want my legacy to be?"

Your organization may not invest in poverty-stricken entrepreneurs or offer internship opportunities to under-served young workers, but you can still connect yourself and your team members to the issues and interests of our broader society. I've found that a powerful way to do this is through team outings. This simply involves gathering your team and leaving your day-to-day corporate context to increase your awareness and appreciation of an organization or individual serving some segment of society.

When my company translated one of our assessment products into braille, I saw an opportunity to make a critical connection. We contracted with the National Braille Press in Boston, Massachusetts, to perform the work. I gathered my product team, and we arranged a tour of the facility. We learned about the challenges facing visually impaired adults and children. We saw the painstaking care with which the workers produced books and media.

We were inspired to learn that the organization received advanced copies of the Harry Potter book series so employees could work around the clock to ensure that visually impaired children would receive their copies on the same day their friends and classmates could purchase traditional versions of the books. We walked away with an expanded awareness of our human condition and a fresh perspective on our place within it.

As a leader, you can connect the dots between your organization's product or service and how it impacts real people in the real world. Too often, we become fixated on what happens inside our physical or virtual walls at work. If your product or service doesn't have a direct tie-in to society, consider taking a team outing to visit an organization or an individual whose society-enhancing work you find inspiring. If your team is remote, host a Zoom meeting with an outside representative as a special guest.

The Nobel Prize may be an annual award, but the fruits of an enlightened leadership approach are available to us every day. Anything we can do to raise awareness of the inherent and profound connectedness we have to all humankind is an act of enlightened leadership. As Acumen's CEO and Founder Jacqueline Novogratz (2010) said from the stage: "Our lives are so short, and our time on this planet is so precious, and all we have is each other."

PLANET

The blue whale's back glistened beneath the powerful California sun. At over eighty-four feet long and nearly fourteen feet high, it was larger than a tractor trailer. Dozens of onlookers surrounded the whale, marveling at its massive size. The enormous whale wasn't breathing. Even so, nobody seemed particularly alarmed.

That's because it was a sculpture.

A pair of artists crafted the life-sized blue whale out of plastic trash collected from the San Francisco Bay area. A blue whale can weigh as much as 300,000 pounds, which is roughly the amount of plastic waste discarded into the ocean every nine minutes (Wright 2018). The Monterey Bay Aquarium commissioned the world record–setting sculpture to raise awareness about the magnitude of plastic pollution in our oceans and its devastating impact on marine wildlife (Guinness World Records, n.d.).

With sufficient commitment and compassion, when we Expand the Circle beyond our species, we reach the level of our planet. Themes we've covered such as connectedness, suffering, and benevolence apply to our planetary home as much as they do to us, its inhabitants. Enlightened leadership capitalizes on our opportunity to mobilize our organizations, teams, and ourselves to prevent or even reverse the negative consequences we often impart on our ecosystem.

Kat Nouri is an entrepreneur who was unsettled by the single-use plastic bags she was depositing into her kids' lunchboxes each week (Raz, Thompson and Grant 2021). She launched the company Stasher, maker of what she describes as a "radically functional, endlessly reusable silicon storage bag" (Cole Haan Brandvoice 2020). Consumers embraced Stasher's simple way to boost sustainability. While growing the company, Nouri secured an investment through the reality funding TV program *Shark Tank* before later selling the company. According to Nouri, her entrepreneurial adventure proved that it's possible to "produce something that is good for people and good for the planet and have it be profitable."

Creating a new venture rooted in sustainability is one thing, but what happens when you're the largest beverage company in the world?

Competing goals present a very real challenge for Coca-Cola as does its staggering scale. The company sells its products in nearly 30 million retail stores across more than 200 countries (The Coca-Cola Company, About, n.d.). Over 1 million Coca-Cola products are purchased every minute. This just in; that's a lot of bottles.

It's also a lot of plastic waste.

According to a complaint filed by one environmental organization, Coca-Cola is the leading plastic waste producer in the world, generating 2.9 million tons of it each year (Global Citizen 2017). While its plastic bottles are designed to be recycled, less than a third actually are. Critics have observed that the company has missed its recycling targets for decades, and consumers have begun to demand more from the multibillion-dollar beverage company (Socio 2021).

Coca-Cola has responded with a slew of sustainability projects. For example, the company is continuing its recycling efforts, but it's also developing bottles made from more eco-friendly alternatives to plastic. According to the company, "The world has a packaging problem. As the world's biggest beverage company, we have a responsibility to help solve it" (The Coca-Cola Company, What is, n.d.) It has also partnered with the World Wildlife Fund on a variety of sustainability and clean water programs ranging from restoring farmland to wildfire suppression to removing invasive plants in regions across the globe (Bonini 2021).

Other companies are doing their part to provide employees with opportunities to serve our planet (Recycle Coach 2020). Clothing maker Patagonia supports employee volunteer efforts that benefit local environmental organizations. A program at Nike's headquarters emphasizes reusable dishware as opposed to disposable lunch containers. Intel provides highly visible e-waste containers to help employees dispose of spent electronic devices.

Leaders at every level can strive for sustainability in other ways. Employees at Unilever, for example, recommended that the company reduce the amount of paper used to seal its tea bags by a mere three millimeters (Polman and Bhattacharya 2016). Compared to the size of a blue whale, three millimeters may seem insignificant, but the paper savings added up to a reduction of more than ten tons of paper. Regardless of your company size or industry, you can always boost your sustainability efforts. You can engage those around to you contribute to constructive projects and programs, and you can connect their efforts to the benefits these practices produce to serve something larger.

Enlightened leadership doesn't stop at the boundaries of work as we traditionally define them. We have a significant dependence on our planet as well as the opportunity and responsibility to serve it well. We have reason to be optimistic. Stasher's Kat Nouri says, "If we can keep creating those moments where we're all proud of what we do and we can create intentionally and with conscience, then I think there's a lot of hope" (Cole Haan Brandvoice 2020).

Even business behemoths bigger than a blue whale can change their attitudes and actions. Echoing the essential themes of an enlightened leadership approach, James Quincey, chairman and CEO of Coca-Cola, observed, "If the pandemic has taught us anything, it's that we cannot act alone. The crisis has shone a light on the interconnected nature of our world" (The Coca-Cola Company, 2020 World Without Waste, n.d.).

BEYOND

Cosmologists have made two important observations about the size of the universe. First, it's more than 92 billion light years in diameter. Second, this figure is almost certainly wrong (Gordon and Tilman 2022).

The universe is believed to be even larger than our limited visibility and calculations can quantify. It may always be. Some barriers simply cannot be crossed.

I refer to whatever lies past the inherent limits to our seeing, knowing, and understanding as *beyond*. In theistic traditions such as Christianity and Islam, beyond is the domain of a supreme being. Idealistic monism holds that a non-being universal spirit or mind is situated beyond our apparent reality. Materialists believe that our perception of reality is a byproduct of physical matter and neurological processes; our consciousness and anything seemingly beyond it is an illusion. Buddhist non-dualism espouses *shunyata,* or emptiness; what lies beyond is ultimate reality in which any phenomenon, object, or individual lacks an intrinsic and enduring self. Of course, even these characterizations are generalizations at best, and heated debates occur between and within each belief system.

I'm glad we got that straightened out.

From an enlightened leadership perspective, squabbling over the unknowable squanders precious time, energy, and the opportunity to liberate ourselves and better serve those around us. Even so, we must recognize that whatever our personal beliefs may be regarding that which lies beyond, we're presented with compelling questions we must reconcile for ourselves. What's the meaning of life? Who am I? What's my purpose?

We rarely raise these existential topics in our day-to-day work. That doesn't prevent them, however, from surfacing and impacting our work and our work experience in subtle and not-so-subtle ways. As presented in earlier chapters, essential themes of connectedness, fear, equanimity, suffering, and benevolence influence how we see the world *and* how we see the world of work. Left unanswered, life's big questions buzz about us like the three Killer Bs, our inescapable needs for Being, Belonging, and serving something Bigger than ourselves.

Now finding ourselves near the end of our exploration, we must return to where it all began: my inevitable death.

You may recall that facing my own mortality is what set me off on this wonderful journey of investigation and discovery. As I came to the final stage of codifying an enlightened leadership approach, I drew inspiration from a wholly unexpected source: near-death experiences (NDEs). Bruce Greyson is a psychiatrist with more than four decades of research experience studying people who have had NDEs following trauma, heart attacks, attempted suicide, and other mortal causes.

Greyson documented his discoveries in his book, *After: A Doctor Explores What Near-Death Experiences Reveal about Life and Beyond*. His research subjects represent a diverse spectrum of ages, nationalities, ethnicities, religious and nonreligious beliefs, and personality types. Most of their NDEs possess several curious commonalities.

In less than an estimated 5 percent of cases, subjects reported having a negative experience such as finding themselves in a sensory-deprived black void (Spectrum Integrators 2022). Fortunately, positive near-death experiences are much more common. In these cases, the subject often reports having had a sense of timelessness, peace, cosmic unity, a profound connectedness to others, or being the recipient of unconditional love.

Remarkably, Greyson also observed powerful transformations in these people's lives that lasted long after their brush with death had ended. "They seem to have increased compassion and concern for others and a sense of connection to—and desire to serve—other people, which often leads to more altruistic behavior. Experiencers tend to see themselves as integral parts of a benevolent and purposeful universe ..." (Greyson 2021, 172) The fact that so many of our themes of enlightened leadership are present in near-death experiences seems beyond coincidence. Considering the resulting peace of mind and personal transformation, it's a shame we can't *all* benefit from their transformative effects.

Having never had a near-death experience myself, I did the next best thing; I simulated one.

During a particularly powerful meditation session, I decided to engage in a contemplative exercise. I imagined that I lost everything in my life. I started mentally letting go of my possessions before moving on to the people I hold dear. I removed my achievements, my health, and my identity. Finally, I ceded my life energy to the best of my ability. While I didn't experience the profound effects of a true near-death experience, what happened next deeply affected me all the same.

As I continued to meditate, I began to bring things back into my life one by one. I didn't force my thoughts or choices, however. I remained still and quietly observed whatever appeared as if I were watching a movie unfold on the silver screen.

> *I'm lying in a hospital bed. I flutter my eyes open. I'm alive. How nice.*

> *A nurse walks into the room. Even better! I ask her how she's doing and how her work is going. She seems mildly frustrated about something, but after a motivational coaching conversation, she leaves the room with a bounce in her step. I smile as I look up at the ceiling.*

> *Suddenly, my bride enters the room, and my heart leaps. I feel incredibly fortunate to still have her in my life.*

> *In her brassy, bottom-line manner, she furrows her brow and says, "You know you can sit up, right?"*

> *I'm delighted to learn that I have full physical functioning. I come to a sudden realization. "You mean I can walk all around the hospital and talk to other people about their work and goals?" I can hardly sit still.*

"Not only that," she continues. "We can leave whenever you're ready."

"I'm going to walk all around town and connect with other people. This is amazing!"

She leans in. "Okay, but are you ready for this? We don't have a lot of money, but we can afford Internet access."

"Wait, what?" I pause in stunned silence. "We can afford the Internet?" I sit for a beat while taking in this shocking revelation. "You're telling me I can connect with people anywhere in the world any time I want, learn about their work, and try my best to help them?"

This exercise revealed two things. First, while I've struggled with poverty mind and measuring up my entire life, what I truly desire is marvelously meager. More importantly, my most pressing priorities are crystal clear and infinitely within my reach. Taken together, these simple truths were simultaneously liberating and inspiring.

This meditation experience illuminated my path to fulfilling my Killer Bs. In that moment, it helped me crystalize my mission to teach leaders to liberate themselves. I came to know who I am more deeply than before. Through sharing my observations and insights with others, I've met incredible people, rekindled relationships, and deepened my connection to those around me. I recognized that when I take an enlightened leadership approach, I make an impact that extends far beyond what I can see, and which will last long after I'm gone.

I had to strip everything away to find my central belief; if I can breathe, I can lead, and so can you.

Tame your Killer Bs. Gain clarity regarding your unique answers to what it means to reach *beyond* to find your innermost sense of *being*, *belonging*, and that which is *bigger* than yourself.

When we Expand the Circle to its widest aperture, we're confronted with all that we cannot know. Rather than see this as a reason for hopelessness or despair, an enlightened leadership approach views our inherent limits as an invitation to increase our mindfulness and our connection to our deepest personal experience. It raises awareness to the opportunity we each have before us. This is the future I see.

Wherever we find ourselves in our vast universe, we embody enlightened leadership. We embrace our unique circumstances and the power they hold for us. We use this unique perspective to guide our artful thoughts and actions. We aspire to benefit others. We amplify our awareness and acceptance of what is here with us now and all that is possible when we Expand the Circle.

* * *

TIPS & TAKEAWAYS

1. **Cross the line.** Be willing to extend your leadership beyond the traditional confines of your organization. Make an impact on the world at large, and let it repay you for your effort.

2. **Be the home team.** Rather than attempt to leave work behind, consider what lessons, tools, and techniques may help you leverage your leadership. A little creativity will go a long way.

3. **Lead local.** Your community is teeming with people who work together to support one another. Bring enlightened leadership into your everyday interactions and exchanges.

4. **Get it together.** While it may seem as if we are separate from one another, we share a common bond of humanity. This is a time when it pays not to mind your own business.

5. **Tread lightly.** We are imposing an increasingly high toll on our planet. Shift the balance by making it a priority to create and participate in sustainability programs and education.

6. **Go beyond.** Don't ignore the existential questions that shape our lives and our work. Push past the boundary and connect with your enlightened leadership potential.

PART II

THE PATH

BECOMING AN
ENLIGHTENED LEADER

———

*I know the price of success: dedication, hard work, and an
unremitting devotion to the things you want to see happen.*

—FRANK LLOYD WRIGHT

My feet were sore. My lower back ached. I was sunburned,
exhausted, and dehydrated. I was moving slowly through the
darkness. My day started well before sunrise, and it wasn't
going to be over any time soon.

I couldn't remember the last time I was so happy.

An Ironman triathlon is an endurance race marked by a 2.4-
mile swim, a 112-mile bike ride, and a 26.2-mile marathon
run. Athletes must complete all three stages back-to-back in
less than seventeen hours to earn the coveted title of "Ironman finisher." After spending just under sixteen hours on
the course in Coeur d'Alene, Idaho, I entered the chute that
led to the finish line. The crowd of spectators and volunteers

cheered wildly. I heard the legendary announcer Mike Reilly call out, "You're an ironman, Matt!" With that, I became one of the world's slowest finishers of one of the world's most iconic endurance races.

My achievement was more than four years in the making. It began when I first learned about the race. The oversized objective seemed incredibly daunting. A part of me doubted that I'd ever be up to the task. A bigger part of me was determined to prove myself wrong.

I began with a self-assessment. I was a painfully slow runner, I didn't own a bike, and I couldn't swim the length of an indoor pool. Okay, this was shaping up nicely.

Undaunted, I doubled down by committing to my aspiration. I wrote out my goal declaration statement, and I enlisted the support of friends and coworkers by telling them about my plan. Several even stopped laughing long enough to help.

I shifted into action mode. I joined a masters swim program led by a patient coach. I visited a cycling specialist who loaded me up with a bike, essential gear, and advice. I acquired a pair of suitable running shoes. I found a few reputable books loaded with week-by-week workouts. These started out simply enough, and they culminated in race-day readiness. I was confident that if I put in the work and stayed on the path, I would achieve my goal. And I did.

While my path to Ironman was clear, my journey as an aspiring leader was anything but.

I found no shortage of leadership development books and articles, but I had no clear path to follow. Without any structure, I was left to make it up as I went along. I was surrounded by supportive people in the form of bosses, peers, and colleagues from other companies. What they provided, however, was loose advice that I had to sort out in my head and translate to my specific work context.

I didn't know where to begin, and while I was putting in the proverbial miles, I was frustrated. I felt like I was trying to build a castle on constantly shifting sands. My personal journey toward enlightened leadership was a zigzag across two decades roaming in the wilderness without having a well-lit path to follow.

I want you to fast forward past my struggles and successes, my painstaking research, and my aha breakthrough. In Part One, I have done my best to illustrate the Expand the Circle framework. Now I want to lay out a path toward becoming an enlightened leader using that framework.

I hope that by lighting the path, I can offer you the same learning opportunities I discovered in my own leadership journey while saving you the time and the frustration I experienced along the way.

The path toward becoming an enlightened leader has the same three steps we saw in my triathlon example:

Assessment >> Aspiration >> Action

Let's briefly examine each of these steps.

Assessment

Without an understanding of where you're starting, knowing how best to get to where you want to go is difficult. To help guide you, I will introduce you to a simple *Assessment* to pinpoint areas where you'd most like to improve. You'll be able to see where you've already developed a basic level of competence and other areas where you need to deepen your leadership capacity.

Aspiration

When you express your intention to achieve something important in your life, you take a pivotal step toward making it a reality. *Aspiration* is about declaring your hope and intention regarding the possibility of becoming an enlightened leader and seeing a pathway to make it a reality. This is the domain of goal setting. In this section, I will give you a powerful goal-setting framework to help you set realistic and achievable goals.

Action

To accelerate your development, I will introduce you to a series of simple yet powerful exercises. By taking *Action* and completing the Expand the Circle exercises, you'll feel yourself making real progress and gaining confidence in your capabilities. You can only become a more enlightened leader by translating intention into action.

When it comes to following the path, you have two options.

Option 1 is linear. In this approach, you can go through all the exercises in the sequence in which I present them. The benefit of this approach is that you'll be certain not to skip any steps. You'll find that each exercise is built on the one that precedes it. You will proceed step-by-step as you Expand the Circle starting with Lead Yourself all the way through Lead the World. It's not the fastest option, but it's the most thorough.

Option 2 is targeted. You can use the results of the personal assessment in the next chapter to identify the specific areas you most want to improve. You can set your goals and aspirations accordingly, and you can focus on the exercises corresponding to your specific improvement areas. You can always go back and tackle a next wave of improvements or pick up on other exercises that you skipped over the first time.

Whichever option you choose, you'll only increase your capabilities if you're willing to put in the work. I have lit the path, but only you can walk it.

By boosting your enlightened leadership, you may experience a variety of benefits including:
- undergoing a positive transformation in the way you think, feel, and act
- knowing that you're truly making progress instead of merely hoping you are
- feeling confident that you're mastering your craft and deepening your leadership capacity
- increasing your connection to those around you
- feeling as if you're keeping up with the career progression of other leaders around you

- raising your visibility inside the organization and your reputation as a capable and respected leader
- creating new opportunities for your advancement and increased responsibility
- enjoying the peace of mind and lightness that comes from doing well *and* doing good

Beyond these personal benefits, you'll have a greater impact on your business, those around you, and the world.

Ready to step onto the path?

Let's begin by discovering where you are now.

ASSESSMENT—
KNOW THYSELF

———

This self-assessment presents questions related to the topics found in each layer of the Expand the Circle framework. Use your responses to raise your awareness to specific layers or elements where you would like to concentrate your focus and improvement efforts. You will find exercises associated with each element in the Action section of this chapter. You can also return to this assessment later to compare your responses to today's baseline.

LEADING YOURSELF

Awareness	Given a blank sheet of paper, I can quickly write out my leadership values, purpose, behavioral style, and weaknesses.	Yes	No
Acceptance	I rarely dwell on my faults and prior failures, and I am quick to forgive myself for any shortcomings that I notice in my thoughts, feelings, and actions.	Yes	No

Confidence	I am thoroughly confident in my leadership abilities across a variety of situations, and despite challenges that may arise, I feel a strong sense that I am worthy of success and happiness.	Yes	No
Authenticity	I know my purpose in life, and I regularly make choices and take actions that are consistent with my true nature, even when it's not easy to do so.	Yes	No
Transcendence	I can easily name recent examples where I made a selfless contribution to the benefit of another, and I regularly feel deeply connected to something bigger than myself.	Yes	No

LEADING OTHERS

Empathy	I regularly pause to consider and appreciate how others may be feeling in each situation, even when those feelings may be difficult or require me to make a change in my approach.	Yes	No
Altruism	I am willing to put myself at risk or expend my time and resources to help another person even when I have no personal gain.	Yes	No
Trust	I readily extend trust to others even early in my relationships, and I engender their trust in return.	Yes	No
Fairness	I am aware of my inherited and conditioned biases, and I regularly take steps to minimize their potential negative effects on those around me.	Yes	No
Connectedness	I avoid setting myself apart from others by recognizing that we are all profoundly connected to one another in terms of our worth and our welfare.	Yes	No

LEADING YOUR TEAM

Vision	I have crafted a clear and compelling vision of the future my team is working toward, and I regularly engage in storytelling to reinforce their enthusiasm and commitment.	Yes	No
Identity	I have taken specific steps to create a strong identity for my team, and I use a variety of tools and ceremonies to reinforce the ongoing value of team membership.	Yes	No
Cooperation	I have created a team dynamic that fosters cooperation and collaboration even in the presence of competing goals, competing styles and needs, and limited resources.	Yes	No
Safety	I foster an environment where team members can make mistakes without fear of undue repercussions, are willing to speak up, and readily ask me and one another for help.	Yes	No
Cohesiveness	I consistently identify and incorporate specific activities and approaches that increase my team's ability to draw closer together rather than be pulled apart over time.	Yes	No

LEADING YOUR ORGANIZATION

Mission	I have clearly articulated my organization's mission, I explicitly communicate it, and I take steps to help employees see themselves supporting it whenever possible.	Yes	No
Culture	I have intentionally and thoughtfully designed my organization's culture, and I have actively shaped our culture through consistent effort and progressive interventions.	Yes	No

Alignment	I have installed a variety of mechanisms to ensure that all parts of the organization are clear about their respective efforts and that each employee can see how their contributions affect the organization's performance and welfare.	Yes	No
Wellness	I'm thoroughly aware of my organization's workplace wellness programs, I model well-being behaviors, and I encourage others to do the same.	Yes	No
Benevolence	I have clearly identified the full range of our organization's stakeholders, and I can specifically describe how we are positively impacting each of their interests.	Yes	No

LEADING THE WORLD

Family	I deliberately try to integrate my work and family life, I repurpose techniques that work in one domain for use in the other, and I reinvest successful experiences across the two.	Yes	No
Community	I employ my leadership skills and techniques in my interactions with members of my community, and I encourage others to do the same.	Yes	No
Society	I am mindful of the connection between my own circumstances and those of humanity, and I directly support people and organizations who benefit society.	Yes	No
Planet	I am aware of the specific impact my organization makes on the planet, and I am active in taking steps to reduce and offset any negative impact that may result from our operations.	Yes	No
Beyond	I regularly practice mindfulness to connect with what lies beyond myself and my subjective experience, and I appreciate the wonders inherent in our world.	Yes	No

ASPIRATION—THE WILL BEFORE THE WAY

Becoming an enlightened leader is a transformative experience. A successful journey requires three key elements I refer to as *know how, can do,* and *want to.*

> *The Expand the Circle framework and examples presented in this book provide the know how you need.*

> *We're each presented with opportunities to practice an enlightened leadership approach nearly every moment of every day, which means any of us can do it.*

> *The aspiration we declare signifies that we want to improve and grow.*

I've studied successful people and organizations for more than two decades. I've primarily done this from a Western perspective with a focus on motivation and goal setting. Early in my career, I learned that to most effectively manifest some desirable future state or outcome, we should strive to set SMART goals. These are goals that are Specific, Measurable, Achievable, Relevant, and Time bound.

Being an insecure overachiever, I extended this guidance by making mine SMARTEST. I now teach leaders to set goals that are Energizing (they should naturally excite and motivate you), Shared (you should be willing to enlist an accountability partner to help you follow through on them), and Trackable (you should be able to document and review your progress toward them over time).

I later studied goal-setting theory at the doctoral level, and I included goal attainment outcomes in my dissertation study of a technology-assisted coaching intervention. My research and practice have demonstrated that goals are important because they are directive, energizing, and conducive to individual, group, and organizational achievement.

From an Eastern perspective, aspiration plays a somewhat different role. When we examine aspiration through this lens, we see that aspiration is a genuine wish to cultivate enlightenment in our leadership. We wish to attain this ideal state to help others whether they are very near to us or at the periphery of our circle of existence. In this view, the very act of expressing sincere aspiration itself produces a positive outcome even before it fuels subsequent action.

Just as the Expand the Circle framework melds Eastern philosophy into Western leadership practice, we can integrate both into our aspiration. We can "feel the wish and form the will." By being mindful about our sincere desire to become enlightened leaders, we boost our motivation, dedication, and perseverance, all of which we will need as we walk the path of personal transformation. Only our aspiration can help us overcome a lifetime of self-oriented leadership habits and conditioned reactions.

Codifying your aspiration by completing the following goal declaration statement can be very helpful:

I will perform [#] acts
in my development of [enlightened leadership element]
on or before [date],
and I will ask [person] to be my accountability partner
as I strive to achieve my goal.

Let's review an example. Sarah is a high-potential individual contributor. She's worked with her manager, Micah, and they've agreed that she tends to withdraw during large group meetings. Her coworker Tamika naturally oozes confidence and is a trusted confidante who attends many of the same meetings. Sarah has set an intention to boost her confidence so that she can rise to meet the leadership moment in this setting.

Sarah's goal declaration statement may look something like this:

I will perform [three] acts
in my development of [confidence]
on or before [my next monthly one-on-one with Micah],
and I will ask [Tamika] to be my accountability partner
as I strive to achieve my goal.

Capturing a goal declaration using paper or pixels can help increase your clarity and commitment, two key drivers of goal attainment.

* * *

You *know how* to Expand the Circle. You *can do* it based on your opportunity and ability to practice enlightened leadership every minute of every day. If you develop your *want to* by cultivating a sincere wish to liberate yourself and serve others, you will prepare yourself to follow through on your aspiration.

Now that your preparation work is complete, you're ready to take action.

ACTION—STEPS
ALONG THE PATH

——

HOW TO LEAD YOURSELF

The aim of enlightened leadership is liberating yourself so you can best serve those around you. This objective must be pursued in a specific order, however. You cannot most effectively serve others until you first learn how to liberate yourself. Therefore, we Expand the Circle from the inside out. The following exercises will help you take your first steps in learning to lead yourself.

AWARENESS

Awareness is the foundation of enlightened leadership. If you lack self-awareness, you won't be able to tap into your strengths or make the most effective decisions. This explains why Tasha Eurich (2017, 5), author of *Insight: Why We're Not as Self-Aware as We Think, and How Seeing Ourselves Clearly Helps Us Succeed at Work and in Life* says that "self-awareness is the meta-skill of the twenty-first century." When coaching leaders, I often help them practice developing self-awareness by exploring their personal values.

EXERCISE: PUMP UP THE VALUE

In this exercise, you will increase your self-awareness by identifying your most closely held personal values.

1. Review the list of values below.
2. Choose your top ten values from the list. If you hold values that are not on the list, simply add them to one of the blank spaces.
3. From your top ten, narrow your values to your top five.
4. From your top five, narrow your values to your top three.
5. From your top three, choose your single most closely held personal value. Which one value would you most like to honor and amplify in your leadership?

Accountability	Empathy	Support
Courage	Enthusiasm	Transparency
Creativity	Humor	Trustworthiness
Dedication	Persistence	Vision
Discipline	Positivity	_____
Efficiency	Resilience	_____

By increasing our self-awareness, we deepen our foundation of what matters most to us. This reveals the origin of our thoughts, feelings, reactions, and how we are showing up as leaders. Enlightened leadership also invites us to develop our mental skills of focus, attention, and concentration.

* * *

ACCEPTANCE

None of us is perfect. If you're like most people, your perceived shortcomings, failures, and negative experiences can diminish your sense of confidence and self-worth, thereby muting the full impact of your leadership. It takes practice, but you can learn to regard yourself with kindness and recognize how even your flaws contribute to your unique leadership presence.

EXERCISE: WHO, WHAT, WHEN

In this exercise, you will identify your specific self-judgment triggers.

Who	Think of a person whose accomplishments, recognition, or status have caused you to discount your own. How would you prefer to view their achievements?
What	Think of a specific characteristic, tendency, pattern of thinking, or behavior you dislike about yourself. How would you prefer to view these parts of yourself?
When	Think of a time when you struggled or failed that caused you to discount your self-worth. How did this experience shape your present understanding and capabilities?

* * *

Enlightened leadership is about accepting the totality of ourselves, including what we consider to be our less desirable characteristics. Ironically, we are often quick to offer understanding and forgiveness to others, while we ruminate on our own shortcomings and failures. When we're able to practice self-acceptance, we unblock the flow of energy, grace, and positivity that will serve those around us as a result. Self-acceptance allows us to fully step into our capacity as enlightened leaders.

CONFIDENCE

Before you can effectively lead others, you must project self-confidence and the sense that you're ready for the leadership moment. This requires self-worth and a feeling that you're able to perform effectively under the specific circumstances. Vigilance pays off here; being able to detect those situations and conditions that run counter to our innate confidence is important.

EXERCISE: MAKE THE SHIFT

In this exercise, you will consider several forces that can erode confidence and how you can remedy them in your leadership.

	Confidence Killer	When and How I Feel It	What I Want to Remember
Imposter syndrome like I'm unworthy of my achievements			
Envy like others have more than me			

	Confidence Killer	When and How I Feel It	What I Want to Remember
Superiority like I'm better than others			
Challenge like others are trying to under- mine me			
Rejection like others don't like me			
Fear like something bad will happen to me			
Taking credit like I must make it mine instead of theirs			

* * *

As leaders, we have a lot at stake. Leading is not easy, and we must both recognize and seize the leadership moment whenever it presents itself. Self-esteem gives us ample leadership capacity. Enlightened leadership requires discipline, effort, and a great deal of persistence. When we actively develop our self-confidence over time, we fill our tanks with the fuel we will need on our long journeys.

AUTHENTICITY

One of the greatest challenges you will face as a leader is to bring your full self into your leadership approach. Whenever you try to put on appearances or hold back a portion of your- self, you minimize your leadership impact. The personal and external consequences of doing so can negatively impact our physical and mental health.

EXERCISE: COMPARE AND CONTRAST

In this exercise, you will reflect on what it means to live with integrity.

1. Think of a recent activity you performed that didn't fully align with your highest sense of purpose, values, and being.
   a. How would you describe your thought patterns while you performed this activity?
   b. How would you describe your emotional response while you performed this activity?
   c. How would you describe the physical state of your body while you performed this activity?

2. Now think of a recent activity you performed that did fully align with that same sense of purpose, values, and being.
   a. How would you describe your thought patterns while you performed this activity?
   b. How would you describe your emotional response while you performed this activity?
   c. How would you describe the physical state of your body while you performed this activity?

3. Compare and contrast the two sets of responses.

* * *

As leaders we wish to be happy and free of suffering, just like those we lead. Accomplishing this requires us to live in a whole and integral way. Enlightened leadership means gaining clarity about what it means to live a life that is in harmony with our true selves. It asks us to demonstrate the courage and discipline to do so even when it's not convenient or easy.

TRANSCENDENCE

Before you can become an enlightened leader, you must reconcile a simple but paradoxical truth: It's not all about you. Despite the mammoth efforts we make toward self-mastery, the pinnacle of our leadership is erasing our relentless focus on our own condition, interests, and circumstances. A tendency toward self-absorption holds back our leadership potential.

EXERCISE: THE BIG PICTURE

In this exercise, you will take a broader perspective and elevate your leadership capacity in the process.

Answer the questions corresponding to each of the sections below.

Person: Who is a person at work or in your life who you thoroughly wish to be successful?	In what ways do you wish them to be free of suffering?	In what ways do you wish them to be happy?

Project: What is a project or initiative that you would like to see be successful?	In what ways do you wish it to prevent negative consequences?	In what ways do you wish it to deliver positive outcomes?
Purpose: What is a movement or a change in the world that you would like to see be successful?	In what ways do you wish it to prevent negative consequences?	In what ways do you wish it to deliver positive outcomes?

* * *

Self-transcendence is about taking perspective from a vantage point higher than yourself. It is not an abandonment of your essence, however, but rather an integration. Through self-transcendence, you enhance your sense of connection with and service to something bigger than yourself. This type of integration allows us to make meaningful and lasting connections with the people and organizational outcomes we aim to lead and serve.

HOW TO LEAD OTHERS

Leading another person is the basic building block of enlightened leadership. To lead others well, we must first make ourselves equal. This type of equanimity creates a powerful connection and prevents us from buying into the delusion that we can be successful when those around us are not. Next, we must exchange our interests for success and happiness with theirs. We want their avoidance of suffering and attainment of happiness ahead of our own. When we lead others in this way, we Expand the Circle of our enlightened leadership.

* * *

EMPATHY

Being human, we're wired to recognize and consider the experiences of others. Empathy is the ability to demonstrate an awareness for and appreciation of another person's subjective experiences. In this way, empathy is a precondition for servant leadership. While we may be preoccupied with our self-interests or concerned about taking on the challenges of others, both parties benefit under a condition of empathy.

EXERCISE: THROUGH THEIR EYES

In this exercise, you will practice empathy by taking the perspective of others.

1. Think of two people with whom you currently work. Choose one person who is currently struggling at work and one who is currently succeeding at work.
2. For each person, reflect on the following prompts using the space provided:
   a. Describe the person's current work situation.
   b. What might they be experiencing?
   c. What may be contributing to their situation?
   d. What advice or observation would you share with them if you knew they would receive it with openness and appreciation?
   e. When and how will you share it with them?

An enlightened leadership approach is an empathetic approach above all. When we practice empathy, we open a door to a deeper level of connection and contribution. We can raise our awareness of others' experiences, and we can engage them directly to learn more about what they are thinking and feeling.

ALTRUISM

Altruistic behavior occurs when you expend resources to another's benefit above your own. When you act in an altruistic way, you help them satisfy their needs and enhance their performance and well-being. Being altruistic isn't always easy, however. When time and resources are scarce or when perceived risk or pressure is high, we often revert to our personal interests and preservation.

EXERCISE: HELPING HANDS

In this exercise, you will explore a time when you demonstrated altruistic behavior.

1. Think about a time when you acted selflessly to benefit another person.
2. What was the situation?
3. What made you choose to act as you did?
4. How specifically did you take action?
5. How did your action benefit the other person?
6. How did your thinking and feeling change as a result?

* * *

When we embrace enlightened leadership, we increase our willingness to demonstrate altruistic behavior. By increasing our awareness of others' needs and taking actions to address them, we place their welfare ahead of our own. This type of servant leadership investment produces outsized results through improved performance and well-being on the part of the individual as well as enhanced satisfaction on our part.

* * *

TRUST

Trust between two individuals is always essential, and for leaders, the trust dynamic is even more critical. According to Stephen M. R. Covey (2018, 5), the author of *The SPEED of Trust: The One Thing That Changes Everything,* "Simply put, trust means *confidence.* When you trust people, you have confidence in them—in their integrity and their abilities." He describes the simple relationship that exists between trust, speed, and cost.

EXERCISE: TIP THE TRUST SCALES

In this exercise, you will examine the conditions resulting from situations involving high and low trust.

1. Think of a relationship in which you and the other person have low trust in each other.
   - In what ways is your speed slower as a result?
   - In what ways are your costs higher as a result?
2. Now think of a relationship in which you and the other person have high trust in each other.
   - In what ways is your speed faster as a result?
   - In what ways are your costs lower as a result?

* * *

An enlightened leadership relationship is grounded in trust. This means that we must both present ourselves as trustworthy and be willing to make the first trusting move. Trust between two people reduces friction and accelerates well-being and performance.

FAIRNESS

Many factors contribute to the inescapable role bias plays in our leadership and our lives. Biology, environmental factors we experienced while growing up, and conditioned responses and beliefs may all work against us. To tame complexity in our world, we often consciously or unconsciously categorize people. A common form of unconscious bias is known as an affinity bias or a preference to associate with others whose demographic and psychographic categories are similar to our own.

EXERCISE: CIRCLE OF TRUST

In this exercise, you will identify and compare the attributes of people with whom you have high trust.

1. Make a list of five people at work with whom you have the greatest level of trust.
2. Identify your personal characteristics in the following dimensions: gender, nationality, native language, accent, age, race/ethnicity, and professional background.
3. Now, compare these same characteristics for each of the people you named in the first step.
4. In what ways are your most trusted connections like you? In what ways are they different from you?

* * *

Fairness is essential for enlightened leadership. Due to prior conditioning, we must take active steps to surface and offset the deeply ingrained associations we may hold about broad categories of people. By raising our awareness of potential bias, we're more likely to embrace fairness and foster greater leadership as a result.

CONNECTEDNESS

Nicholas Christakis and James Fowler observe that "our connections affect every aspect of our daily lives." An invisible yet powerful interconnectedness binds us all, for better or worse. According to Christakis and Fowler (2011, 30), "We rarely consider that everything we think, feel, do, or say can spread far beyond the people we know."

EXERCISE: TEN TIMES TEN

In this exercise, you will reflect on your ten most frequent connections and their extended connections.

1. Choose the ten people with whom you interact most frequently and significantly during an average week.
2. What do you know about *their* ten closest connections?
3. Imagine that you, your top connections, and all their top connections were together at a party. What might you notice?

* * *

Enlightened leadership requires us to overcome our traditional perceptions of separateness and recognize that we're inherently connected to one another. Any notion that we can insulate ourselves from those around us is illogical and counterproductive. Fortunately, this means that our enlightened leadership is itself contagious. When we properly lead those around us, we expand the benefits far beyond our limited visibility.

HOW TO LEAD YOUR TEAM

When we Expand the Circle beyond a single individual, we are ready to lead a team. Small groups of people can accomplish more together than a single individual, but the need for awareness, insight, harmony, and balance increases exponentially in line with our responsibility as leaders.

VISION

An enlightened leader defines the direction for their team. The first step in being able to do this well is to analyze what's on the horizon. In their book *Illuminate: Ignite Change Through Speeches, Stories, Ceremonies, and Symbols*, communications experts Nancy Duarte and Patti Sanchez (2016, 9) write that "leaders anticipate the future. They stand at the edge of the known world, patrolling the border between 'now' and 'next' to spot trends." Once you've seen the future and have designed the plan to reach it, you must next turn your attention to translating your vision into a vehicle for your team's effort and enthusiasm.

EXERCISE: STORY TIME

In this exercise, you will capture the main story elements relating to an important effort at work.

1. Think of a significant project, deliverable, process, or initiative that you are a part of at work.

2. Answer the questions corresponding to each storytelling phase below.
   a. Adventure
      ii. What is the motivation that drove the effort?
      iii. What are the negative consequences of doing nothing?
   b. Challenge
      i. What challenges and roadblocks stand in the way?
      ii. What is the cost or risk of failure?
   c. <numbered2>Victory
      i. What positive state will be achieved upon successful completion of the journey?
      ii. How will the organization, team, or group be transformed as a result?

* * *

Leading your team begins with painting a clear picture of your transformation story. This is essential not just for clarifying the work to be done but also for enhancing aspiration and excitement among your team members. Remember that enlightened leadership is about bringing others along with you.

IDENTITY

Humans are socially driven, and we have a need for affiliation. Your ability to enhance long-term team membership and loyalty is critical to both the performance and experience of your team members. By creating a clear and compelling team identity, team members will be more committed to remaining a member of the team and to exerting commitment and effort toward the team's objectives and welfare.

EXERCISE: NAME THAT TEAM

In this exercise, you will evaluate the identity of the teams you are a part of and how these identities could be even more compelling.

1. Think of three teams that you are currently a part of at work or in your personal life.
2. For each team, how strong is the team's identity on a scale of one (low) to ten (high)?
3. What would enhance each team's sense of identity and belonging?

* * *

When we create a strong sense of identity and affiliation for our teams, we meet our team members' social needs and we perform better as a collective whole. Simple practices and ceremonies can go a long way toward developing and preserving a team's identity and fulfilling team members' needs for belonging and to serve something bigger than themselves.

COOPERATION

Your success as a leader depends in large part on how well you can orchestrate the collective efforts of a diverse team. Many team objectives and types of team compositions naturally invite competing goals and competing styles. You will need to overcome these opposing forces to ensure that team members work together in pursuit of the team's goals and the collective welfare of all stakeholders.

EXERCISE: GET IT TOGETHER

In this exercise, you will identify your contribution to and benefit from a team.

1. Identify a team on which you're currently playing an active role.
2. Complete the following table.
   a. (Columns) What do you give to the team? What do you get from the team?
   b. (Rows) Knowledge, Skills, Abilities, Resources

* * *

An enlightened leadership approach fosters collaboration and cooperation among team members. By reducing or removing the "me" issues that naturally arise in conventional team situations, you will be able to enhance the team's experience while delivering outsized results. Many organizational forces present a negative influence on cooperation. Remain committed to cooperation to navigate your team through choppy waters.

SAFETY

Amy Edmondson (2019, 8) describes psychological safety as "the belief that the work environment is safe for interpersonal risk taking." Your success as a leader will be constrained if you're not able to foster an environment of safety in a way that supports team member well-being but also lays the groundwork for performance.

In this exercise, you will identify the role safety plays alongside performance in the team dynamic.

1. Identify several teams that you are a part of.
2. For each team, identify which quadrant best describes the current team situation.
   a. Low Performance, Low Safety
   b. Low Performance, High Safety
   c. High Performance, Low Safety
   d. High Performance, High Safety
3. For each team that is not in the "High Performance, High Safety" quadrant, what might you do to nudge the team dynamic "up and over"?

* * *

If team members don't feel safe, are afraid to speak up for fear of repercussions, or are hesitant to share their observations or suggestions, increased suffering is the inevitable result. An enlightened leadership approach is one where team members feel supported and secure when they may otherwise perceive risk and negative consequences.

COHESIVENESS

Just as properties in the physical world allow molecules to stick together, certain properties in the organizational world create cohesion within and among our teams. When you foster an environment of cohesion, team members are pulled together by a seemingly magnetic force. Belongingness and performance are both enhanced as a result.

EXERCISE: STICK TOGETHER

In this exercise, you will reflect on how the team dynamics you've experienced help or hurt group cohesion.

1. Think about three to five teams where you played a significant role at work or in your personal life.
2. Name five team dynamics that served to push team members away from one another.
3. Name five team dynamics that served to draw team members toward one another.
4. How can you specifically take action to affect your current team dynamic in a way that prevents pulling apart and encourages drawing together?

* * *

By taking an enlightened leadership approach, we channel the energy present in our team members as a force that draws us closer together regardless of what circumstances we may face. In fact, preserving cohesiveness during challenging times can be the most rewarding and memorable type of team experience we can have. Obstacles are teachers. Use them to hone your enlightened leadership skills by amplifying your ability to draw people together when they would otherwise be pulled apart.

HOW TO LEAD YOUR ORGANIZATION

Our organizations are thriving, dynamic social networks of enterprise. When we Expand the Circle to the level of the organization, we look for ways to institutionalize our enlightened leadership. When we create organizations that are as intent on employee welfare as they are on producing results, we reach the next level of our leadership potential.

MISSION

The reason your organization exists is a powerful motivator. Simon Sinek (2009, 15) highlights a leader's accountability when he shares that "every instruction we give, every course of action we set, every result we desire, starts with the same thing: a decision." You can choose to bypass this critical step or proceed with only a vague sense of organizational purpose. The right choice, however, is to get clear on your WHY.

EXERCISE: SAY WHY

1. Imagine that a prospective investor, customer, or employee wants to work with your organization.
2. In ten words or fewer, how would you convey your organization's WHY to them?
3. On a scale of one (low) to ten (high), how consistently is your organization delivering on your WHY? What organizational change would increase your rating?

* * *

Every employee—like every leader—experiences a pressing need to be a part of something beyond our limited self-interests. Leaders then are in the best position to declare and articulate the purpose that drives the organization. Sinek (2009, 215) notes the power of possibility. "Every company, organization, or group with the ability to inspire starts with a person or small group of people who were inspired to do something bigger than themselves."

CULTURE

Your organization's culture constitutes an environment in which employees and teams thrive or languish. As the former chief talent officer of Netflix, Patty McCord discovered that while culture can become a catalyst for business and individual success, talking about it is easier than building it. According to McCord (2017), "Most companies are clinging to the established command-and-control system of top-down decision making but trying to jazz it up by fostering 'employee engagement' and by 'empowering' people."

EXERCISE: CHANGE IT UP

In this exercise, you will identify a new behavior or capability that will better align your culture with your aspirations.

1. Consider your long-term aspirations for your organization as well as what new or different capabilities you will need to adopt to reach your objectives.
2. What is a specific organizational behavior, attitude, dynamic, or capability that you would most like to instill?
3. Which department or group may be best suited to first make this change?
4. What role can you play in initiating the necessary culture change?

* * *

An enlightened leadership approach recognizes the influence that an organization's culture has on its employees and seeks to create an environment that serves workers and the bottom line. Within your own circle, you need to take active steps to bring, develop, and maintain an intentional culture.

ALIGNMENT

A big part of a leader's job is ensuring that the work flows through the organization—up and down, across, and inside out—as freely as possible. Alignment allows various parts of the organization to achieve and maintain a type of synchronization in their respective activities and interests. Ensuring that employees directly see the impact of their efforts on the organization's mission is essential.

EXERCISE: FALL IN LINE

In this exercise, you will evaluate your organization's current alignment infrastructure.

1. On a scale of one (low) to ten (high), rate your organization's current proficiency in the following aspects of your operating infrastructure:

   a. Transparency—employees can clearly see how their contributions relate to the organization's mission and priorities.

   b. Measurement—progress and performance are quantifiable and trackable rather than subjectively conveyed by senior management.

   c. Integration—cross-functional objectives minimize the likelihood of competing goals that pull employees apart.

   d. Participation—alignment isn't seen solely as a top-down prerogative but also as a bottom-up invitation to define the organization's focus and investment.

   e. Dialogue—the organization facilitates open discourse on matters of creating, adjusting, and maintaining alignment in ways that serve both employee and business interests.

* * *

When we create alignment, we increase the likelihood of success for our organizations and our people. At an organizational level, speed and efficiency increase in lock step with alignment. On an individual level, being able to directly see the impact of one's efforts also connects them to the organization's larger mission.

WELLNESS

While most organizations offer some form of wellness programs, participation rates among employees are often low. According to Laura Putnam (2015, xxvii), "Just having a wellness program is not enough, and having an ill-conceived wellness program is often worse than not having one at all." As a leader, you have an opportunity to enhance the well-being of your employees through your influence and intention.

EXERCISE: GET WELL SOON

In this exercise, you will identify and evaluate your familiarity with and mobilization of organizational wellness.

1. Identify two to three workplace wellness programs offered by your organization.
2. Evaluate your employees' active participation level in these programs. (If you're not directly familiar with these figures, partner with a knowledgeable HR partner.)
3. Choose an existing program in which you would like to see more participation or a new program element that you would like to introduce.
4. Identify key influencers from various parts and levels of the organization who can help you contribute to the program's success.

* * *

Enlightened leadership aims to serve its employees just as they serve the organization through their efforts and contributions. Therefore, being a strong advocate for workplace wellness is important. Putnam highlights this opportunity, writing, "Leadership is, perhaps, the most critical factor in determining the success of any workplace wellness initiative."

BENEVOLENCE

Leaders have a responsibility to make an impact beyond the bottom line. Lynn Sharp Paine recognizes that this is a shift from previous attitudes. She writes, "Through their activities as decision makers, organization builders, and societal leaders, they have the power to make the world not only more prosperous, but also more just and more humane" (Paine 2003, 245).

EXERCISE: RAISING THE STAKES

In this exercise, you will identify the types of contributions your organization is making beyond its local interests.

1. For each of the following groups of stakeholders, name one explicit way in which your organization is advancing their welfare beyond a baseline commercial organizational arrangement.
   a. Investors
   b. Employees
   c. Customers
   d. Communities

* * *

Enlightened leadership broadens the definition of performance to include benevolence that serves a variety of external stakeholders and not merely the interests of the organization itself. This is becoming a welcome trend. Paine writes that "a high-performance company that competes unfairly, mistreats employees, or neglects its civic role is becoming a contradiction in terms."

HOW TO LEAD THE WORLD

When we have reached the pinnacle of our leadership ability, we are prepared to Expand the Circle to the farthest reaches we can imagine. Our leadership efforts can spill over into our families and communities, benefit society and our planet, and connect us deeply with that which lies beyond our ability to know and understand with certainty. Leading the world stretches us to become and to give the very best of ourselves.

FAMILY

If you have a bad day at work, keeping that negativity away from home is difficult. At the same time, the challenges and commitments of family life inevitably impact your work. Rather than create artificial barriers, you must seek a deeper integration between both domains.

EXERCISE: FAMILY TIES

In this exercise, you will explore how family experiences shape your work experiences.

1. Think of how a parent, grandparent, guardian, or caregiver described their work when you were growing up. What are your earliest memories of work?
2. Based on your present attitudes, behaviors, and descriptions of your work, what impression is your family receiving about your work experiences?
3. What would you most like your family to know about your work experience in the future?

* * *

If we can resist the urge to compartmentalize work and family life, we open ourselves to new possibilities. Taking an enlightened leadership approach means borrowing techniques from the workplace and bringing them home with us. This also means working toward harmony and integration rather than artificially trying to keep these domains apart.

COMMUNITY

We live and work in our local communities, but we rarely think to bring our leadership outside of the work context. When you stop to consider what a leader does—envision a positive future state, demonstrate empathy, actively listen, motivate others, act in a way that raises others' welfare—it becomes clear that you have ample opportunity to extend your leadership into your community if you're able to shift your perspective.

EXERCISE: COMMUNITY LEADER

In this exercise, you will identify opportunities to enhance your leadership in your community.
1. Think of two to three examples of regular interactions you have with members of your community. These

could be everyday places like the grocery store or the dry cleaner or community organizations such as civic clubs and associations.

2. Answer the following questions for each.
   a. What is my current leadership attitude and behavior when I interact with these community members?
   b. In what ways could I enhance my positive impact through those interactions?
   c. How can I remind myself to show up as a leader the next time I have the opportunity to do so?

* * *

Enlightened leaders are "always on" to the best of our abilities, even in our communities outside the workplace. The context or setting matters less than our intention and execution. Even a small act such as inquiring about a community member's well-being or offering a compliment can radiate positivity through our communities and have an impact far beyond what we're able to directly witness.

SOCIETY

We are united by our human condition, and many groups face specific challenges or need help in easing their suffering or promoting their well-being. Consider the experience of Jacqueline Novogratz, CEO of the socially oriented venture capital firm Acumen. In *The Blue Sweater: Bridging the Gap between Rich and Poor in an Interconnected World*, she wrote that her experiences working to reduce global poverty "allowed me to believe we could—and therefore must—create a world in which every person on the planet has access to the resources needed to shape their own lives" (Novogratz 2010).

EXERCISE: HIGH SOCIETY

In this exercise, you will identify specific organizations that serve a human-interest population that resonates with you.

1. Think of a specific aspect of the human condition that you are particularly interested in or experience deeply rooted compassion for.

2. Identify one or more organizations or groups who actively serve those needs in society.

3. Consider making a connection with one of the organizations to learn more about what they do and how you may support their efforts.

4. Consider sharing what you've learned with your team members and encourage them to engage in a similar exercise.

* * *

When we engage to help the more distant members of our human family, we increase our sense of connectedness and belonging in a deeply satisfying way. As Novogratz observes, "Today we are redefining the geography of community and accepting shared accountability for common human values." An enlightened leadership approach therefore invites us to reclaim our connection to all of humanity.

PLANET

By our very nature as living beings, we consume ecological resources. We have an opportunity and a responsibility to offset this consumption by acting as good stewards of the planet. Sustainability is more achievable than ever, and you can overcome the often-unconscious one-way relationship we have with the earth's resources in a variety of ways.

EXERCISE: HOME SWEET HOME

In this exercise, you will identify current sustainability programs offered by your organization.

1. List the sustainability programs offered by your organization.
2. Answer the following questions.
   a. What is the current level of awareness regarding these programs?
   b. What is the current level of participation in these programs?
   c. What might you do to increase awareness and participation where needed?

* * *

An enlightened leadership approach asks us to reexamine our relationship with the planet that sustains us. By raising our awareness and taking small actions that add up over time, we can reduce our impact on the environment. As a secondary benefit, by taking sustainable actions, we're able to reconnect with nature and enhance our sense of wonder at its beauty and dynamic essence.

BEYOND

Sometimes we're faced with existential questions that cannot be answered through conventional means. Rather than ignore them or defer them for another more convenient time, we can deepen our connection with what lies beneath our current level of day-to-day awareness and consciousness. In doing so, we can derive benefits that directly manifest in our leadership capacity, well-being, and wisdom.

EXERCISE: MIND THE GAP

In this exercise, you will simply experience being mindful and fully aware of the present moment.

1. Set a timer for ten minutes.
2. Sit comfortably yet attentively with your hands in your lap or resting on your knees.
3. Close your eyes.
4. Focus your attention on your breathing, noticing how your chest and abdomen rise and fall with each breath.
5. If a thought comes to mind, resist any urge to engage with it or to pass judgment; silently stay "thinking" to yourself and return your attention to the breath.
6. Settle into the present moment and your awareness until the timer sounds the end of your session.

* * *

The path to becoming an enlightened leader begins and ends with pure awareness and being mindful of the present moment. While we may each have different views, beliefs, and opinions about what lies beyond our existence, mindfulness offers us a way of experiencing this transformative practice that is found in most ethical, moral, and contemplative traditions.

PART III

THE LAMP

LIGHTING A LAMP FOR OTHER LEADERS

———

If you light a lamp for someone else it will also brighten your path.

—*BUDDHA*

One morning, a manager received a text message from a team member that read:

> *"Wanted to thank you for your thought leadership and pushing our team to be our very best. I feel myself growing every single day under your leadership."*

How do you think the manager felt after reading that text message? I would use terms such as energized, appreciative, and connected. I might also say proud and warm.

I should know. *I* received that text message.

I was honored and humbled to be on the receiving end of my team member's sentiment. I share it here for two reasons. First, I've had the great fortune to study enlightened leadership and try my level best to practice its approach as outlined in this book. Second, the leaders where you work can absolutely make a similar impact on those around them if they do the same.

How would your organization be different if every leader practiced the enlightened principles included in the Expand the Circle framework? How would your culture and the well-being of your workers change for the better? How would your business results improve, and how would your extended stakeholders' benefit?

These changes won't happen on their own, but they can when you light a lamp for other leaders.

I've been fortunate to do this with peers, direct reports, and through organization-wide leadership development programs. Simply put, nothing is more rewarding than helping others grow their leadership capacity and make a larger impact on the business and those around them.

As you experience the personal benefits of an enlightened leadership approach, you will likely want to share your enthusiasm and newfound insights with other leaders around you. If you're able to bring leadership development to your organization, I recommend you do so in the following phases:

1. PRACTICE

Make it a point to fully absorb the framework yourself and apply the techniques and lessons to your own day-to-day leadership. By gaining direct experience with the material and techniques, you'll increase your conviction around introducing an enlightened leadership approach in your organization. Putting yourself in the best position to lead by example is important.

2. PITCH

None of us is the sole decision maker when it comes to introducing leadership development into an organization. Even business owners need to secure commitment from their leaders; anything less will "fail in the field." You may need to create a business case to secure the full investment of time and resources a program will require. If so, refer to the proof points associated with the elements included in the framework such as improved retention, increased innovation, and productivity gains.

3. PLAN

Develop answers to some basic questions to increase your likelihood of success. Who specifically will participate in this leadership program? For example, you may consider experienced leaders, aspiring leaders, or both. How will you engage your leaders? Options range from book clubs to weekly team huddles to monthly large group discussions. What tools will you use to support the effort? I've included some examples on my personal website, which is referenced in the Resources section.

4. PILOT

In larger organizations, beginning with a small group of leaders at first can be very helpful. For example, beginning with the executive leadership team can create top-down buy-in. Another option may be to choose particularly entrepreneurial teams or those having a specific interest in leadership investment. A pilot program can allow you to build momentum, demonstrate small wins, and garner support before a broader deployment.

5. PROPAGATE

When you're ready for a full-scale deployment, maintaining visibility is key. Transformation programs fade over time far too frequently without reinforcement. You will also want to manage expectations. Leadership investments produce substantial results, but they require changing mindsets and behaviors which can take time. Be sure to celebrate wins along the way to sustain positive momentum.

If you can exercise your own enlightened leadership and apply yourself when manifesting the attitudes and the techniques listed in this framework, you will put yourself in the best position to light the path for other leaders who are on your team. In doing so, you will cascade your leadership and send ripples of benefit, positivity, and impact through your team members, into your organization, and out into the world at large.

* * *

TIPS & TAKEAWAYS

1. **Care to share.** Enlightened leadership can transform your approach, but you don't have to stop there. Engage other leaders and invite them to step onto the path as well.

2. **Make it personal.** Take the time to fully immerse yourself in the framework and exercises. This will put you in the best position to support others when they follow your lead.

3. **Take the stage.** Be prepared to connect the dots for decision makers. Use your organization's current challenges and opportunities to highlight the framework's business benefits and corresponding elements.

4. **Plan for success.** Develop a clear set of answers to the most pressing questions. Who will receive training, how will you introduce it to them, and what materials will support the program?

5. **Start small.** Consider beginning with a small-scale pilot program. Your executive leadership team or a particularly progressive team leader may be ideal places to get things moving.

6. **Think big.** After you've built sufficient momentum, keep going. Enlightened leadership is an approach needed by leaders at every level, and its benefits are just as universal.

TIPS FOR EXECUTIVES

———

As an executive, you are well positioned not only to person-ally reap the benefits of an enlightened leadership approach but also through the work of level down leaders across your organization. You have three significant advantages in this regard. First, your voice is heard the loudest, and you can rise above the noise that otherwise drowns out novel ideas and opportunities. You're also the chief decision maker when it comes to investments of time, money, effort, and attention. Finally, you establish the priorities for your organization.

It's surprising, therefore, that so many executives struggle to give leadership its due. Many reasons contribute to this. A closer look reveals that the average executive is exceptionally busy; it seems everybody wants a bit of your time or a smack-erel of your attention. Executives have also been trained to seek short-term returns on investments, making it difficult for people-centric programs to make the cut. Leadership development investments can also be difficult to quantify, leading some executives and their CFOs to raise their eye-brows when a big-ticket development program lands on the docket without a well thought out business case.

As if these challenges weren't formidable enough, there's the seismic shift in our world of work to contend with. Executives are navigating digital transformation, supply chain problems, cybersecurity, a long-term shift toward remote work, and sustainability (Wiles 2022). Even on the people front, important investments must be made in talent acquisition; retention; succession planning; and diversity, equity, and inclusion (DEI), among others.

With so many priorities competing for an executive's attention, where does leadership land on the agenda?

"I think about this all the time," said Henry Schuck, founder and CEO of ZoomInfo, a rapidly growing go-to-market intelligence company. In an interview, he explained, "It's probably the biggest thing I think about. Do I have the right leadership team in place to get us to a new place or to continue in the positive direction that we're going?" His focus on leadership has paid off; ZoomInfo doubled its annual recurring revenue between 2019 and 2021 and crossed the billion-dollar mark in 2022 (Nasdaq, n.d.).

Since growing ZoomInfo to more than 3,000 employees, Schuck now thinks about his organization's leadership capacity in layers. "What is our leadership directly underneath me, and then what is our leadership one level below that and one more level below that?" Considering the company's size and rapid growth, top-down leadership is critical. He's seen the direct relationship between leadership and business performance over and over.

"When there's a problem in the business, my first thought is, have we had and do we have the right leadership in the organization to solve those issues? Why or why not? If we don't, what are we doing to solve for that?" This analytical approach makes a critical connection. While many executives fixate on external market conditions, competitor capabilities, or operational issues, Schuck looks to a more central source:

"Every problem in the business is a people problem."

"Anytime there's an issue in the business, you can see that's an area that we haven't invested in from a leadership perspective. In the areas that are going really well, those are the areas where we've really invested." This explains why the company puts so much effort into propagating its cultural values, collecting feedback, and conducting a variety of development programs for its 500-plus leaders (Kruse 2022).

Schuck didn't always appreciate the critical role of leadership, however. "I used to think that if you hire really great people, they don't really need to be managed." He quickly realized that leaders have an important role to play in influencing the mindset, performance, and experience of those around them. "Today, I really believe that leaders bring out the best in their people."

Looking to the future, ZoomInfo shows no signs of slowing its growth rate. Schuck stressed the importance of investing in leadership at every level of the organization when he concluded, "I think it's pretty clear that our managers are the single biggest leverage point in the company. Having great managers and leadership across the company is what can really drive leverage, better operating efficiency, and just a better organization."

Leadership plays a central role in any organization's long-term success. Executives, therefore, need to create the conditions for successful leadership development.

Richard Sheridan is the cofounder, CEO and chief storyteller of Menlo Innovations, a software and IT consulting firm. Menlo has been widely recognized for its positive workforce environment. Senior leaders visit Sheridan and his leadership team to observe the company in action and to glean his insights. He highlights the importance of taking a thoughtful approach when building culture. "If you're going to be intentional about your culture, you better be intentional about the leadership within that culture," Sheridan told me in an interview.

When taking on a leadership development effort, executives need to cultivate an environment for successful transformation. According to Sheridan, "I see this broken down into three big categories: purpose, permission, and practice." Purpose relates to the WHY that is driving the effort. Participating leaders at every level must understand the intention of the program and the outcomes it's expected to achieve.

Sheridan has had the most success when he highlights the external impact of a culture shift. He poses the question, "Who do we serve, and what would delight look like for them?" His inside-out focus will be very familiar to those looking through an enlightened leadership lens. "If you start from an aspect of serving those external to the organization—even beyond our customers, our employees, and our shareholders to include the world—I think that can be very inspiring but also informative to people about how we should treat each other."

Permission is the next critical element in Sheridan's approach. He recognizes that if you are attempting to make a material shift, "you've got to give people some space to try stuff." He knows from experience that fear destroys organizational will and follow-through. To offset this risk, executives must create psychological safety by explicitly giving permission to make the change.

The final pillar in Sheridan's framework is practice, or "the idea of giving people space to deliberately practice new leadership skills." For Sheridan, leadership transformation isn't only about having leaders take a class or read a book. It requires actively creating opportunities for deliberate practice across the organization. This is the only way to lock in the lessons and new mindset and behaviors.

Any type of organizational change is difficult, and increasing leadership capacity is no exception. This type of personal transformation can be even more challenging in dynamic markets, in organizations that are under pressure to perform, in mature organizations, and in organizations having a poor culture. According to Sheridan, the human aspect of change also presents challenges. "When you're talking about change, you're talking about people changing their behaviors. That's a hard thing to do."

Sheridan suggests an often-overlooked executive tool during times of change: rewards and recognition. "People will hang on to even pain-filled reward systems because in the face of change, they're being asked to trade something they know for something they don't know." Just as we saw fear undermine so many of the enlightened activities in the Expand the Circle framework, it can prevent even the most beneficial change. As an executive, recall that culture is what we reward and punish. If we want to help our leaders take on new attitudes and behaviors, we're going to need to introduce new rewards to support the shift.

What's most important when introducing leadership development improvements is to remain positive. This relates to your positive intent, attitude, and determination over time. In his book *Chief Joy Officer: How Great Leaders Elevate Human Energy and Eliminate Fear,* Sheridan (2018, 247) writes, "If you approach business—if you approach the hard work of leadership—with positivity, you will reap great rewards."

As an executive, you're ultimately accountable for your organization's leadership capacity. You have a unique opportunity, therefore, to advance enlightened leadership not just for your own benefit but also for that of your employees, your bottom line, and your community of stakeholders.

When you light a lamp for your leaders, your organization can do well *and* do good.

* * *

TIPS & TAKEAWAYS

1. **Take charge.** Use your elevated position to bring enlightened leadership into your organization. Be an active and visible supporter for your aspiring leaders as they look to you to set the example.

2. **Look around.** Remember that business issues are indications that a better leadership approach is needed. Give your level down leaders the resources and support they need to rise to the challenge.

3. **Take advantage.** Gain leverage by increasing leadership capacity throughout your organization. Look to leadership to create better operating efficiencies, more flexibility, and an attractive landing spot for high performers.

4. **Set the stage.** Create the conditions that will allow leaders at every level to perform at their best. Provide mechanisms where leaders can learn and apply new skills without fear of failure.

5. **Give it time.** When it comes to people, fast is slow and slow is fast. For any of us, changing longstanding patterns of thinking and doing is difficult, so strive to be patient and celebrate continuous improvement.

TIPS FOR TEAM
LEADERS

———

As a team leader, you've been rewarded for your track record of achievement and dependability. You recognize, of course, that your team's performance isn't automatically a reflection of your natural strengths and abilities, however. Your leadership as well as that of your team members is required for collective success.

You can develop the leadership capacity of your team in three primary ways. First, you can—and should—lead by example. Your team members are always watching, and they're taking careful notes about your attitudes and behaviors. Second, a team member may approach you for advice. They may be interested in specific books, articles, courses, mentorship opportunities, or other resources that align with their development needs.

Your third option—proactively bringing leadership development opportunities to your team—is the most powerful but also requires the most finesse. You may observe a gap in performance, communication, team-oriented behaviors, or some other opportunity to raise your collective game. Or perhaps you just want to be a good steward for the learning and growth of your team members. Whatever the reason, at some point you will find yourself wanting to light a lamp for them.

What's the ideal mindset for a team leader who's intent on developing their team members?

"How can I help make this person as successful as they can be?" asks Ann Yauger. She's the AVP, Product at CarMax, the nation's largest used vehicle retailer, headquartered in Richmond, Virginia. In an interview, Yauger explained, "When you enter the relationship with a lot of humility for yourself and a lot of commitment to them, you don't ask, 'What is this person doing for me?' but instead, 'What do I need to do to help make them successful in the business and in their own career goals? How do I make them feel confident?'"

Yauger relies on a variety of techniques to accomplish her development goals. For example, she meets with each team member once a week. During these one-on-one sessions, she asks her two favorite questions: "What's going on?" and "How can I help you?" The responses allow her to tailor her development approach and offer coaching specific to each person's needs and objectives. She recognizes that she may need to bend a bit to accommodate their work style, not have them adapt to hers.

Yauger also uses targeted sessions to delve deeper. "Once a month we do an hour-long meeting that's focused solely on their development." She uses this time to connect personal growth opportunities with their work. She'll ask, "From a business standpoint, what do you think were your biggest wins and biggest opportunities this month?" This business context frames the individual's performance, experience, and action.

To highlight additional opportunities, she poses another thought-provoking question to her full team. "'What are all the things we want to get better at as a team?' We're always working on one development area that we've identified together in addition to something that's important to conquer for each leader's next-level development." A team environment built on trust and safety invites the entire team to surface areas of need and to offer coaching and support to one another whenever a topic is put forward.

"People can learn so much from each other, and it's important for them to be comfortable asking for help, and giving help, to make them a stronger leader," Yauger noted. She shared a recent example when a less experienced team member brought a next-level leadership need to the meeting and asked if the others had advice or experiences to share. "We all went around and shared stories and ideas, and everybody got a lot out of it." It was so popular; it became a regular part of team meetings. "A year later, somebody else came into the meeting with a similar problem, and it was cool to see that this person now took the lead on helping someone else with that same issue."

Yauger recognizes that her team doesn't operate in a vacuum; a bigger picture exists beyond simply doing great work. She demonstrates an enlightened mindset when she says, "I feel like I have this additional goal of being a leader of our culture. I want everybody to love working here. I want everybody to want to come to work every day and rave about it."

"How can we make sure that we're working in a place where people really enjoy what they're doing?" She poses this question to herself and to her team members. "Part of that is knowing that the company really cares about our people and wants them to be happy and wants them to be fulfilled inside and outside of work. There's a good vibe that you get when you work in a place where you feel like you're working with a lot of really caring people who are invested in you."

By making team members part of the process, you boost their autonomy and follow-through. You may even provide a spark that ignites transformation.

Drew Fortin is the CEO of Lever Talent, a talent strategy agency he founded after leading sales and marketing teams in a variety of high growth industries. In his early days of building out a marketing team, he recognized the need to invest in the leadership of his team members. At the time, Fortin and I were peer leaders at The Predictive Index. I had a front row seat as he lit a lamp for his team members in the critical interpersonal area of trust.

Fortin read Patrick Lencioni's book *The Five Dysfunctions of a Team: A Leadership Fable* on a recommendation from another executive. He was struck by the critical role trust plays in the foundation of a functional team dynamic. In an interview, he later told me, "That realization sent me on a journey of how to build trust."

What happened next really struck me.

I started seeing the "trust triangle" from Lencioni's book appear on all the whiteboards in our office. I recognized it from having read the book earlier, but I discovered that Fortin had really run with it with his team. "I don't think you can say it enough, present it enough, draw it enough. I would open every meeting having one of our team members walk us through it. I believed that just the presence of it would give people permission to go into the conflict zone." His disciplined reinforcement let the team know that this wasn't the latest inspiration that would soon wear off. Fortin was committed to building trust over the long haul. The biggest risk was complacency. "Even if we thought we had trust, we didn't have *enough* trust."

Fortin's decision to instruct his team members to present the trust framework to one another was deliberate and had a long-term payoff. "Practice makes permanent," he insisted. The requirement to actively present the material naturally led each team member to really absorb it. Fortin upped the stakes. He had each team member rate their perception of the team's dynamic. "Just to hear other people go through it and rate our current level of trust, conflict, etcetera, was engaging in conflict."

By using existing meetings and events as an opportunity for leadership development, he automated the learning process.

He also elevated the conversation up out of the tactical day-to-day of the business. "The act of presenting something that really has nothing to do with the tasks we're working on today gave people a way to dip their toe in the water." It can be easier at first to examine leadership development concepts and frameworks outside of the work context before connecting those dots.

After a few months of deliberate application, Fortin was approached by a team member who said, "Drew, I don't think we need this anymore." Fortin responded, "Okay, great. Let's not do it for a few weeks and just see what happens." When the company received some employee engagement results that showed room for improvement, the team member approached Fortin again.

"We need to bring the trust triangle back."

That triangle remains a regular fixture in Fortin's strategy presentations, monthly and weekly team meetings, and one-on-one conversations. Fortin's experience demonstrates that, for team leaders, finding creative ways to get team members the development support they need is most important.

For team leaders, success begins with recognizing the leadership moment. You've now discovered an enlightened leadership framework that can serve the business, your individual team members, your organization, and the world that lies beyond the boundaries. Your team members' performance and experience must remain in focus, but by showing them how to Expand the Circle, you invite them to meet their often-unspoken needs and send out ripples of enlightened leadership that impact those around them.

When you light a lamp for other leaders, you show them that it's possible—and essential—to stretch previously limited definitions of success, achievement, and happiness.

* * *

TIPS & TAKEAWAYS

1. **Stay close.** Take advantage of your proximity to your team members. Give them continuous feedback and support as they do the hard work of translating what they're learning into practice.

2. **Open the door.** In addition to your own observations, check in with your team members to find out what development opportunities excite them the most. Giving autonomy will increase their enthusiasm and follow-through.

3. **Join forces.** Look for team-oriented improvements that will allow everybody to work together in each area of development. The team may have some members who do this well and can serve as mentors.

4. **Bring it in.** When you've been inspired by something that helps you raise your game, consider sharing it with your team. Doing so provides a common objective and a shared experience.

5. **Put it on repeat.** Moving on to the next pressing demand can be tempting. Professional growth takes time, however, so be sure to reinforce development exercises and topics until they become automatic.

TIPS FOR HR LEADERS

—

As a Human Resources leader, you play a critical role in helping your organization and leaders at every level perform at their collective best. Whether your function is referred to as Human Resources, People Operations, Talent, or Culture, you sit at the intersection of business and people. Leadership is what makes that critical connection.

Considering how big a job HR leaders have, one might think that you'd get more attention, resources, and respect. I know far too many HR leaders who struggle to get time on the executive agenda. Others find that when the purse strings tighten, their department is the first to feel the pinch. Still others are treated far too tactically, right up until a people problem arises in the business that can't be avoided any longer. That's when the distress call goes out.

Before you can light a lamp and bring leadership development into your organization, you should consider two key viewpoints: how you see yourself and how others see you.

"Almost nobody gets into HR intentionally; it sort of happens organically." Tracie Sponenberg is the chief people officer (CPO) at The Granite Group, a New England-based distributor of plumbing, heating, cooling, water, and propane supplies. In an interview, she expanded on her origin story. "I am one of the very few people who planned an HR career while I was still in high school. I knew HR—or Personnel as it was called at the time—combined my love of people, my real interest in business, and my interest in psychology, which is what I studied as an undergraduate."

Many people are drawn to HR because of its focus on employee welfare. As Sponenberg explains, "The function was created to protect people because employees were literally dying on the job." Unfortunately, many leaders outside of HR think of the function tactically or solely in terms of compliance. Some small business owners, for example, continue to avoid bringing full-time HR representation into their companies for as long as they can.

Sometimes it takes a global pandemic to shake things up.

Sponenberg described how an overnight shift in employee health and safety, remote work, and flexible work led to a mindset reboot for some executives who now thought to themselves, "I wish we had one of those HR people to help us through this thing that nobody has ever figured out how to do before." This created a silver lining of sorts. "The importance of the HR function has really been elevated in places where it wasn't already," she said.

As she looks ahead, she sees more changes coming. "One big trend I'm seeing is that if you Google *chief people officer jobs*, you'll see far more of them than if you look for *chief human resources officer* [CHRO] results." As we saw previously in the Identity section, names matter; they influence how we see ourselves and how others see us. According to Sponenberg, "I want the term to fit the department, and I want the term to fit the business. For us, we call our people '*people*,' not resources, capital, or assets."

For senior people leaders, the nature of the work is also decidedly different than it was in years past. "The HR function has evolved to be more about coaching and consulting, so that's something that I've always done," Sponenberg said. Considering the massive changes taking place across the world of work, it's important to have that type of strategic counsel.

She reflected, "The biggest shift I've seen is that, at least at companies like ours, we're used to saying 'Here's the job. Here's the workplace. If you don't like it, see you later.' And what we've really had to do over the past several years is adapt to the person." This change in approach goes well beyond the hiring phase. "We're looking at every individual and what they need throughout the life cycle of their entire time at the company and trying to match an experience that is unique and personalized for them."

Today, Sponenberg speaks openly to audiences about the transformation she's made going from a tactical compliance-focused HR specialist to how she described herself to me when we first met: "a strategic business leader who happens to work in HR."

Once you've been able to see yourself in the proper light, you're faced with the next objective of making sure others see you in a similarly elevated way.

Berta Aldrich is a C-suite executive whose experience has spanned marketing, strategy, and human resources roles. Her diverse experience gives her a unique perspective on how HR leaders can advance leadership development in partnership with line of business executives.

Partnership with business executives begins with getting clear on the need to act. As Aldrich told me in an interview, "CEOs are going to need different skillsets than those that are currently in the organization today. They have to then be forward-looking and be able to solve for the future." Strategic workforce planning and succession planning can shine a light on the need for additional leadership capacity and a need for a fresh leadership approach. HR leaders are often asked whether the organization has the leadership capacity needed to execute the strategic intent. If the answer is no, you play a critical role in bridging the gap.

Even when the need is clear, creating a business case for the development investment is still important. When thinking about what that business case needs to include, Aldrich says, "I think number one, it has to actually solve for something." She's found success in gaining executive support by producing a clear Return on Investment (ROI). This can often be a high-level view of the mechanics of an expected return as opposed to a down-to-the-penny detailed projection full of assumptions. Preparing the hard business case can grab the

CEO and CFO's attention above and beyond the intuitive need to invest in leadership development.

Aldrich has enough experience to expect obstacles along the way. One of the major risks to garnering support from executives is the dreaded *lip service*. If you hear, "Yes. I know it's a good thing. I know we should be doing it," but if the executives don't *actually* spend time and money on the program, it's going to fizzle. If executives don't at least encourage their people to participate, it will create a missed opportunity.

Another major risk comes from *executive ego*. While the Expand the Circle framework is based on a foundation of selflessness, the exact opposite tact has propelled some executives to the success they enjoy today. As a result, letting that go can be difficult. This is unfortunate, as "they're really doing their teams a disservice," according to Aldrich. In extreme cases, a lifelong CEO may have such an ego-dependency that they may silently wish that their company will struggle at least a little bit after they retire. Although others may be suffering, the executive's ego is delighted by feeling needed.

As an HR leader, taking ownership of your responsibility to develop leadership capacity is important, even in the face of such friction and pushback. According to Aldrich, "The best chief human resources officers (CHROs) are strong, strategic CHROs. They're not tactical. They don't get bossed around. They truly believe that they are in charge of their people as a strategic asset." This mindset can build the motivation and momentum needed to persevere in the face of opposition whether it be from lip service, executive ego, or the status quo. As Aldrich (2021, 150) puts it in her book *Winning the Talent Shift: Three Steps to Unleashing the New High Performance Workplace*, "the head of HR should have ultimate authority and accountability to exercise leadership over the human capital."

For an HR leader, every moment is a leadership moment. When you apply the lessons of this book through your own leadership, you will experience the power and the benefit of a more enlightened approach. Don't be surprised if you transform the way you see yourself and how others see you along the way.

You can be the bridge that makes the critical connection between business and people outcomes, performance and experience, executives and their team leaders, and team leaders and their individual contributors. You have what you need to align your organization's mission, culture, and execution. You can't do these things alone, however. None of us can.

Therefore when you light a lamp for other leaders, you lead the way for us all.

* * *

TIPS & TAKEAWAYS

1. **Fight for your right.** As senior talent leaders, you play an important but sometimes overlooked role. While technical business matters often take center stage, do everything you can to create a people-first perspective.

2. **Ride the wave.** Executives are paying significantly more attention to people issues that affect the business. Take advantage of the shift by being strategic and opportunistic in your approach.

3. **Connect the dots.** Leverage your unique position by having a consulting mindset. Ask thoughtful questions about the business and look for those areas where an enlightened leadership approach could pay dividends.

4. **Look ahead.** Rather than fixate on the here and now, imagine how the organization will need to operate differently in the future. Ask executives and other senior leaders which skills will be needed to get there.

5. **Follow the money.** Even a well-intentioned investment in leadership development needs a strong financial foundation. Use what you know about the business to create a before-and-after picture that highlights the expected return.

PART IV

THE FORMULA

BOOSTING ENLIGHTENED LEADERSHIP CAPACITY

I struggled mightily in my high school physics class. I read the thick, musky textbook chapter detailing the electromagnetic spectrum, but I couldn't wrap my brain around the principles.

The teacher grabbed an item from his desk drawer and beckoned the class to follow him into the hallway. He instructed one of the students to kneel and hold down the end of what looked like an extra-long Slinky, a tightly coiled metal toy. The teacher stretched the coil several feet down the hallway and began to rhythmically shake its far end. Using this physical prop, he demonstrated how waves can have different amplitudes or different frequencies. After the presentation, the textbook formulas had context for me, and I was able to put the lessons into practice.

In the preceding chapters, I've shared many principles and examples of the elements in an enlightened leadership approach. Increasing our capacity as enlightened leaders is nearly within our reach. We just need a final formula:

$$\text{Enlightened Leadership Capacity} = \frac{\text{Mindfulness} + \text{Compassion} + \text{Wisdom}}{\text{Self-Interest}} \quad \Uparrow \quad \Downarrow$$

SELF-INTEREST

From our earliest days as infants, we're taught to discriminate between what comprises ourselves versus the world around us. Your first word was unlikely "I" or "me," but your sense of self has been reinforced since the beginning. Unfortunately, this type of ego orientation can be difficult to outgrow. We see it in "me before we" leaders who always seem to be looking out for themselves or their own objectives.

Our new world of work asks leaders to be more selfless than ever before. We now look to hire, promote, and follow leaders who are empathetic, good corporate citizens, servant leaders, and coaches. Even our organizations are moving beyond self-interest through Corporate Social Responsibility (CSR) and the pursuit of Conscious Capitalism. Overcoming our neurobiology and conditioning to minimize our self-interest is not easy, but we must strive to do exactly that if we're to embrace an enlightened leadership approach.

MINDFULNESS

For me, mindfulness is about awareness, presence, and allowing circumstances and experiences to unfold naturally. When we act habitually, we lack awareness. Becoming preoccupied with past slights or becoming gripped with anxiety about the future pulls us away from the present moment. When we force ourselves to think and act in certain ways, we create friction. Each of these reduce our enlightened leadership capacity.

Mindfulness can be practiced and developed in many ways. I maintain a meditation practice, for example, but even this includes a variety of techniques. You may prefer yoga or long, contemplative walks in nature. Perhaps you have an engrossing hobby or enjoy listening to music. You may turn to spiritual reading or prayer as your go-to when it comes to mindfulness. The "right" technique is the one that works best for you.

COMPASSION

Every worker in every organization wishes to experience well-being and not to experience suffering. When we hold a sincere intention for this wish to be a reality for ourselves and for others, that is compassion. We must first want this for ourselves. While counterintuitive, this can be extremely difficult for some people. I used to be notoriously hard on myself whenever I made a mistake or revealed some shortcoming to the outside world. Through greater awareness and practice, I learned the lightheartedness and benefits that come with self-compassion.

We must likewise learn to extend compassion to those around us. Not just to our families, to our own team members at work, or to coworkers who we like—or those who are most like us—but to everyone. Just as each of us wishes to be healthy, safe, and content, we must likewise develop this wish for them.

WISDOM

To develop wisdom, thinking like a scientist is helpful. We start by making careful observations regarding the world around us. Next, we examine our discoveries by peering in to take a closer look using our natural curiosity and ability to think critically about what we find. Finally, we create connections that unlock our next level of understanding, and we consider how our newfound perspective can help us think, feel, and act in powerful new ways.

In the natural world, optics and acoustics involve producing waves of light and sound unimpeded by obstacles or resistance. In our new world of work, enlightened leadership involves producing waves of mindfulness, compassion, and wisdom unimpeded by an overactive self-interest.

* * *

Looking back, we can see that we've covered a great distance on our journey together.

We set the stage for our discovery by acquainting ourselves with a three-part definition of enlightened leadership. This evolved approach asks us to open ourselves to new beliefs and practices that are simultaneously inspired by ancient wisdom and grounded in modern science.

We met a sugar-spilling philosopher, altruistic humpbacks, and identical twins having uncanny connections. We drew lessons from our quarks, our cosmos, and unexpected sources in between. Dozens of research studies showed us how the elements of an enlightened leadership approach can drive important business outcomes such as increased job performance, innovation, and profitability. We also reviewed research that shows how a more inclusive, engaging, and happier workforce is also ours to cultivate.

We mobilized our newfound practices through awareness, aspiration, and action. We learned how to invite other leaders to step onto the path so we can magnify our collective ability to do well and do good. Finally, we have just seen how timeless principles interact in a simple, actionable equation we can use to increase our enlightened leadership capacity as well as that which is present in our relationships, teams, and organizations.

Pause for a moment to ponder what's possible and what's next. The future is unwritten; it can be as big and bright as you are willing to make it. Any desirable future state, however, can only be created by passing through the present moment. Your very next interaction can reflect an enlightened leadership approach if you're willing to seize the opportunity.

Right now, you have everything you need to send out wave after beneficial wave as you Expand the Circle.

RESOURCES

———

Please visit my website to find additional content, tools, and reference materials:

http://www.mattpoepsel.com/circle

Once you're there, you'll find:
- Book club discussion questions
- Guided meditation tracks aligned with the book's themes and topics
- Professional development templates
- Leadership development program plans
- Links to additional references and reading lists
- and much more!

ACKNOWLEDGMENTS

—

I am incredibly fortunate to have so many supportive people in my life.

To my beloved family: My bride, Tanya, who always seems to know when to ground me and when to lift me up. My daughter, Willa, who kept a watchful eye on my mental health throughout the writing process. My son, Ben, who fueled my curiosity about our world both natural and supernatural. My daughter, Maris, who is the very best antidote to writer's block a creator could ever ask for. My parents, Joe and Mary, for their unconditional love and support.

To the writing and publishing teams at Creator Institute and New Degree Press: Eric Koester for his vision and relentless drive, John Saunders for his creativity and passion, and Shanna Heath for her infectious enthusiasm for the writing process. I'm especially indebted to my editor, Zach Marcum, who saw my book even before I could. Thank you, my friend, for walking the path with me.

To the subject matter experts who set aside their valuable time to be interviewed for the book: Ann Yauger, Berta Aldrich, Blanka van Raalte, Charkie Quarcoo, Chris Dyer, Drew Fortin, Emily Mias, Hema Crockett, Henry Schuck, Marcel Schwantes, Maribel Olvera, Michelle Penczak, Richard Sheridan, Simone Alicia, Tracey Bromley Goodwin and Holly Oberacker, and Tracie Sponenberg.

To the supporters who participated in my pre-order campaign and fueled the enlightened leadership movement: Abby Donnelly, Adesubomi Plumptre, Adrienne Guerrero, Alexa Matarazzo, Alexandra LeBlanc, Allen Lieberman, Alphonso Cheponis, Amy Leslie, Amy Saenger, Andrea Mulligan, Anthony Walley, Bhushan Desai, Bill Betcher, Blanka van Raalte, Brant Boyd, Brett Unzicker, Brian Carrender, Bruce Reading, Caroline Nuttall, Cassandra Smalley, Chauna-Kaye Pottinger, Chris Failla, Chris Palmer, Christina Ghayori, Christine Nast, Christy Green, Connor Jackson, Connor Lewis, Damon Clark, David Langevin, David Sweet, Deborah Watts, Debra Vasques Bruneau, Delaney Valente, Diana Rivenburgh, Dominique MacDonald, Donna Star, Drew Fortin, Emily Mias, Eric Koester, Erin Balsa, Erin Sutton, Erinne Tripp, Frank Hunnewell, Ginger James, Greg Barnett, Greg Turnquist, Gregg Flecke, Hamed Altamami, Harry Layman, Heather Raye, Hema Crockett, Henry Saniuk, Holly DePalma, Jason Astacio, Jason Porter, Jason West, Jeff Leisawitz, Jennifer Liharik, Jennifer Mackin, Jennifer Migliore, Jennifer Tokatyan, Jenny Moebius, Jill Berg, Jim Speredelozzi, Joe O'Brien, John Saunders, Joseph King, Josh Berry, Karen Baird, Karen Blair-Lamb, Karl Francel, Karmen Zabron, Kathleen Teehan, Kathy Weaver, Ken Silber, Kevin Schmitz, Kim Pfluger, Kourous Rezaei, Lalig Musserian, Larissa Haynes, Laura Caton, Laura Morrison,

Lawrence Urbano, Lee Pichette, Len DiSalvatore, Lisa Comley, Lisa Perez, Liz Palmieri-Coonley, Luis Piecho, Mamta Buch, Marcia Bonacci, Maribel Olvera, Mark Rudolph, Mary Beth Hardy, Mary Poepsel, Megan Antonelli, Megan Patel, Melanie Wood, Meri Stockwell, Mher Mardoyan, Michael Mosel, Michael Pogany, Michael Wolfgang, Michele Barry, Michelle Jackson, Michelle Kozin, Michelle Westfort, Mike Olender, Mike Sadler, Mike Stringer, Nancy Martini, Natalia Cheb, Nathan Eatough, Nibal Petro Henderson, Noel DiBona, Olivier Aries, Patrick Reilly, Patrick Rivers, Rabih Shanshiry, Ray Davey, Richard Geremia, Rick Lacasse, Roberta Dombrowski, Robyn Knox, Ron Garfield, Sara Best, Sara Fraim, Scott Burgmeyer, Scott Burns, Scott White, Sean Cavaliere, Sentari Minor, Sergiu Simmel, Shane Reddemann, Shannan Hanson, Shannon Howard, Shawn McCauley, Sherri Gray, Silvia Pardo, Skip Massengill, Sri Chellappa, Stephanie Affentranger Kveton, Stephen Flower, Suzy ElFishawy, Teri Kinsella, Thad Peterson, Tina Bento, Todd Kokoszka, Tom Meusel, Tracie Sponenberg, Tricia Holliday, Trisha Davis-Gray, Ursa Klancnik, Val Yaw, and Zach Schaefer. You each helped make this possible.

Special thanks to The Predictive Index, HR Leadership Group of Northeast Ohio, and Predictive Success Corporation for your generous support.

To my musical muses for scoring the book's soundtrack: Ben Poepsel, Claire Meli, Jack Forrester, Maris Poepsel, and Zach Raye.

To all the above individuals and any others I may have overlooked, I am grateful to have you in my Circle, and I am honored to be in yours.

REFERENCE LIST

———

INTRODUCTION

Goldberg, Emma. 2022. "A Two-Year, 50-Million-Person Experiment in Changing How We Work." The New York Times. https://www.nytimes.com/2022/03/10/business/remote-work-office-life.html (accessed October 15, 2022)

Harter, Jim. 2022. "U.S. Employee Engagement Drops for First Year in a Decade." Gallup. https://www.gallup.com/workplace/388481/employee-engagement-drops-first-year-decade.aspx (accessed October 15, 2022).

Huffington, Arianna. 2014. *Thrive: The Third Metric to Redefining Success and Creating a Life of Well-Being, Wisdom, and Wonder.* London: WH Allen.

Lyra Health. n.d. "The 2022 State of Workforce Mental Health." Corporate Wellness Magazine.com. Accessed October 15, 2022. https://www.corporatewellnessmagazine.com/article/the-2022-state-of-workforce-mental-health.

Maslow, A. H. 1943. "A Theory of Human Motivation." *Psychological Review* 50, no. 4 (July): 370–96. https://doi.org/10.1037/h0054346.

Maurer, Roy. 2022. "Job Openings, Quits Set New Records." SHRM. Accessed October 15, 2022. https://www.shrm.org/resourcesandtools/hr-topics/talent-acquisition/pages/jolts-quits-rate-great-resignation-turnover-march-2022.aspx.

Rinpoche, Sogyal, Patrick Gaffney, and Andrew Harvey. 2002. *The Tibetan Book of Living and Dying.* San Francisco, CA: HarperSanFrancisco.

Smet, Aaron De, Bonnie Dowling, Marino Mugayar-Baldocchi, and Bill Schaninger. 2021. "'Great Attrition' or 'Great Attraction'? the Choice Is Yours." McKinsey & Company. Accessed October 15, 2022. https://www.mckinsey.com/business-functions/people-and-organizational-performance/our-insights/great-attrition-or-great-attraction-the-choice-is-yours.

Tomb, Devin. 2022. "72% Of MUSE Survey Respondents Experienced 'Shift Shock.'" The Muse. Accessed October 15, 2022. https://www.themuse.com/advice/shift-shock-muse-survey-2022.

Wiles, Jackie. 2022. "Employees Increasingly Seek Value and Purpose at Work." Gartner. Accessed October 15, 2022. https://www.gartner.com/en/articles/employees-seek-personal-value-and-purpose-at-work-be-prepared-to-deliver.

THE NEW WORLD OF WORK

ADP, 2022. "ADP Research Institute® Reveals Pandemic-Sparked Shift in Workers' Priorities and Expectations in New Global Study." ADP Media Center. https://mediacenter.adp.com/2022-04-25-ADP-Research-Institute-R-Reveals-Pandemic-Sparked-Shift-in-Workers-Priorities-and-Expectations-in-New-Global-Study (accessed September 3, 2022).

Dhingra, Naina, Andrew Samo, Bill Schaninger, and Matt Schrimper. 2021. "Help Your Employees Find Purpose—or Watch Them Leave." McKinsey & Company. https://www.mckinsey.com/business-functions/people-and-organizational-performance/our-insights/help-your-employees-find-purpose-or-watch-them-leave (accessed September 3, 2022).

Korn Ferry. 2021. "Future of Work Trends in 2022: The New Era of Humanity." https://www.kornferry.com/insights/featured-topics/future-of-work/2022-future-of-work-trends (accessed September 3, 2022).

Kornfield, Jack. 1994. Buddha's Little Instruction Book. *New York: Bantam Books.*

Mental Health America. n.d. "Mind the Workplace." Accessed September 3, 2022. https://www.mhanational.org/mind-workplace.

National Parks Service. n.d. "Grand Canyon: Fossils." Accessed September 3, 2022. https://www.nps.gov/grca/learn/nature/fossils.htm.

PwC. 2022. "What 52,000 people think about work today: PwC's Global Workforce Hopes and Fears Survey 2022." May 24. https://www.pwc.com/gx/en/issues/workforce/hopes-and-fears-2022.html (accessed September 3, 2022).

LEAD YOURSELF

Addicott, Adam. 2020. "Even Serena Williams Has Confidence Issues Sometimes." UBITENNIS. https://www.ubitennis.net/2020/09/even-serena-williams-has-confidence-issues-sometimes (accessed October 15, 2022).

Axelrod, Ruth H. 2017. "Leadership and Self-Confidence." In: Marques, J., Dhiman, S. (eds) Leadership Today. Springer Texts in Business and Economics. Springer, Cham. https://doi.org/10.1007/978-3-319-31036-7_17.

Beck, Martha. 2021. *The Way of Integrity: Finding the Path to Your True Self.* New York: Penguin Life.

Berman, Laura. "Martha Beck and the Way of Integrity." The Language of Love with Dr. Laura Berman, May 26, 2021. Podcast, MP3 audio, 58:51. https://podcasts.apple.com/ca/podcast/martha-beck-and-the-way-of-integrity/id1552549384?i=1000523142360.

Bonenti, Charles. 2022. "Art Under the Microscope: Real or Fake." Art New England. Accessed August 13, 2022. http://artnewengland.com/ed_picks/art-under-the-microscope-real-or-fake/.

Bracht, Eva M., Fong T. Keng-Highberger, Bruce J. Avolio, and Yiming Huang. 2021. "Take a 'Selfie': Examining How Leaders Emerge from Leader Self-Awareness, Self-Leadership, and Self-Efficacy." *Frontiers in Psychology* 12: 635085 (March): 1-12. https://doi.org/10.3389/fpsyg.2021.635085.

Campbell, Jessica. 2022. "Serena Williams on Finding Self-Confidence and Support Both on and off the Court." Women's Health. https://www.womenshealth.com.au/serena-williams-on-finding-self-confidence-and-support-both-on-and-off-the-court (accessed October 15, 2022).

Cunningham, Brittany Packnett. "How to Build Your Confidence—and Spark It in Others." Filmed June 17, 2019, in Vancouver, BC. TED video, 13:21. https://www.ted.com/talks/brittany_packnett_how_to_build_your_confidence_and_spark_it_in_others.

Denmark, Kenneth L. 1973. "Self-Acceptance and Leader Effectiveness." *Journal of Extension* 11, no. 4 (Winter): 6-12. https://archives.joe.org/joe/1973winter/1973-4-a1.pdf

Einola, Katja, and Mats Alvesson. 2021. "The Perils of Authentic Leadership Theory." *Leadership* 17, no. 4 (August): 483-490. https://doi.org/10.1177/17427150211004059.

Eurich, Tasha. 2017. "Increase Your Self-Awareness with One Simple Fix." Filmed December 19, 2017, in Denver, Colorado. TED video, 17:18. https://www.ted.com/talks/tasha_eurich_increase_your_self_awareness_with_one_simple_fix.

Ferriss, Tim. "Tim Ferriss and Brené Brown on Self-Acceptance and Complacency". YouTube. February 10, 2020. Educational video, 7:22. https://m.youtube.com/watch?v=znRLbEcFrRU.

Frankl, Viktor E. 1966. "Self-Transcendence as a Human Phenomenon." *Journal of Humanistic Psychology* 6, no. 2 (Fall): 97–106. https://doi.org/10.1177/002216786600600201.

Frankl, Viktor E., Ilse Lasch, Harold S. Kushner, and William J. Wnislade. 2015. *Man's Search for Meaning*. Boston, MA: Beacon Press.

Gates, Anita. 2018. "Where Art Forgeries Meet Their Match." The New York Times. https://www.nytimes.com/2018/05/02/arts/art-forgeries-sothebys.html (accessed October 15, 2022).

George, Bill. 2015. "Authentic Leadership Rediscovered." HBS Working Knowledge, November 10. https://hbswk.hbs.edu/item/authentic-leadership-rediscovered

Gervais, Michael. "Dr. Tony Nader: Become Your Ultimate Self Through Transcendence." Finding Mastery, November 24, 2021. Podcast, MP3 audio, 1:38:09. https://podcasts.apple.com/us/podcast/dr-tony-nader-become-your-ultimate-self-through-transcendence/id1025326955?i=1000542901396.

Glazer, Robert. "Dr. Tasha Eurich on Building Self-Awareness." *Elevate with Robert Glazer*, July 20, 2021. Podcast, MP3 audio, 46:56. https://podcasts.apple.com/be/podcast/dr-tasha-eurich-on-building-self-awareness/id1454045560.

Hayes, Steven C. 2020. *A Liberated Mind: How to Pivot toward What Matters.* New York: Avery, an imprint of Penguin Random House LLC.

Kanter, Rosabeth Moss. 2005. "How Leaders Gain (and Lose) Confidence." *Leader to Leader* 2005, no. 35 (Winter): 21–27. https://doi.org/10.1002/ltl.110.

Kenrick, Douglas T., Vladas Griskevicius, Steven L. Neuberg, and Mark Schaller. 2010. "Renovating the Pyramid of Needs." *Perspectives on Psychological Science* 5, no. 3 (May): 292–314. https://doi.org/10.1177/1745691610369469.

Kipnis, David, and William P. Lane. 1962. "Self-Confidence and Leadership." *Journal of Applied Psychology* 46, no. 4 (August): 291–95. https://doi.org/10.1037/h0044720.

Koltko-Rivera, Mark E. 2006. "Rediscovering the Later Version of Maslow's Hierarchy of Needs: Self-Transcendence and Opportunities for Theory, Research, and Unification." *Review of General Psychology* 10, no. 4 (December): 302–17. https://doi.org/10.1037/1089-2680.10.4.302.

Levinson, Martin H. 2007. "Reviewed Work: The Myth of Self-Esteem: How Rational Emotive Behavior Therapy Can Change Your Life Forever by Albert Ellis." *ETC: A Review of General Semantics* 64, no. 1: 89. http://www.jstor.org/stable/42578704

Lusianingrum, Farah Putri, and Claudius Budi Santoso. 2022. "The Influence of Authentic Leadership on the Performance of Tasks." *International Journal of Human Resource Studies* 12, no. 1 (February): 56-70. https://doi.org/10.5296/ijhrs.v12i1.19472.

Maslow, Abraham H. 1968. *Toward a Psychology of Being.* Princeton, NJ: Van Nostrand.

Moore, Don A. 2021. "Perfectly Confident Leadership." *California Management Review* 63, no. 3 (May): 58–69. https://doi.org/10.1177/0008125621992173.

Moshavi, Dan, F. William Brown, and Nancy G. Dodd. 2003. "Leader Self-Awareness and Its Relationship to Subordinate Attitudes and Performance." *Leadership & Organization Development Journal* 24, no. 7: 407–418. https://doi.org/10.1108/01437730310498622.

Nader, Tony. 2021. *One Unbounded Ocean of Consciousness: Simple Answers to the Big Questions in Life.* AGUILAR. Kindle.

National Parks Service. "'The Greatest Dam in the World': Building Hoover Dam (Teaching with Historic Places)." U.S. Department of the Interior. Accessed August 13, 2022. https://www.nps.gov/articles/-the-greatest-dam-in-the-world-building-hoover-dam-teaching-with-historic-places.htm.

"Optimizing Authentic Leadership." *Development and Learning in Organizations: An International Journal* 36, no. 2 (2022): 54–56. https://doi.org/10.1108/dlo-06-2021-0107.

Owens, Bradley P., and David R. Hekman. 2012. "Modeling How to Grow: An Inductive Examination of Humble Leader Behaviors, Contingencies, and Outcomes." *The Academy of Management Journal* 55, no. 4. http://www.jstor.org/stable/23317615 (accessed October 15, 2022).

Perry, John. 1979. "The Problem of the Essential Indexical." *Noûs* 13, no. 1 (March): 3–21. https://doi.org/10.2307/2214792.

Ribeiro, Neuza, Ana Patrícia Duarte, and Rita Filipe. 2018. "How Authentic Leadership Promotes Individual Performance." *International Journal of Productivity and Performance Management* 67, no. 9: 1585–1607. https://doi.org/10.1108/ijppm-11-2017-0318.

Ruti, Mari. 2014. *The Call of Character: Living a Life Worth Living*. New York: Columbia University Press.

Samadi, Andrea "Dr. Simone Alicia, the Self-Esteem Doctor on 'Self-Esteem: Why We Must Have It to Succeed'.", Neuroscience Meets Social and Emotional Learning, December 4, 2021. Podcast, MP3 audio, 34:48. https://www.listennotes.com/podcasts/neuroscience-meets/dr-simone-alicia-the-self-DUdLg14k-uT/.

Sounds True. 2020. "Steven Hayes PhD: Self-Acceptance and Perspective-Taking." YouTube. August 3, 2020. Educational video, 44:03. https://m.youtube.com/watch?v=XltTkaUHJxo.

Subramanian, Samantha. 2018. "How to Spot a Perfect Fake: The World's Top Art Forgery Detective." The Guardian. https://www.theguardian.com/news/2018/jun/15/how-to-spot-a-perfect-fake-the-worlds-top-art-forgery-detective (accessed October 15, 2022).

United States Bureau of Reclamation (USBR). "The Colorado River and Hoover Dam - Facts and Figures." Accessed August 13, 2022. https://www.usbr.gov/lc/region/pao/faq.html.

Viktor Frankl Institute. n.d. "Viktor Emil Frankl." Accessed August 13, 2022.
https://www.univie.ac.at/logotherapy/biography.html.

Walumbwa, Fred, Bruce Avolio, William Gardner, Tara Wernsing, and
Suzanne Peterson. 2008. "Authentic Leadership: Development and
Validation of a Theory-Based Measure." *Journal of Management*,
34, no. 1 (February): 89-126.
https://doi.org/10.1177/0149206307308913.

Whitmore, John. 2009. *Coaching for Performance: GROWing People,
Performance and Purpose: The Principles and Practice of Coaching
and Leadership.* London: Nicholas Brealey.

Williams, Serena. 2019. "Serena Williams on International Women's Day:
'We Must Band Together to Fight for What's Fair'." Fortune.
http://fortune.com/2019/03/08/serena-williams-international-
womens-day (accessed October 15, 2022).

Worth, Piers, and Matthew D Smith. 2021. "Clearing the Pathways to
Self-Transcendence." *Frontiers in Psychology* 12:648381 (April).
https://doi.org/10.3389/fpsyg.2021.648381.

LEAD OTHERS

Ben-Ami Bartal, Inbal, David A Rodgers, Maria Sol Bernardez Sarria,
Jean Decety, and Peggy Mason. 2014. "Pro-Social Behavior in Rats
Is Modulated by Social Experience." *eLife* 3:e01385.
https://doi.org/10.7554/elife.01385.001.

Bloom, Paul. 2010. "The Moral Life of Babies." The New York Times.
https://www.nytimes.com/2010/05/09/magazine/09babies-t.html
(accessed October 15, 2022).

Burey, Jodi-Ann. 2020. "The Myth of Bringing Your Full, Authentic Self
to Work." Filmed November 2020 in Seattle, WA. TED video 15:23.
https://www.ted.com/talks/jodi_ann_burey_the_myth_of_bring-
ing_your_full_authentic_self_to_work.

Christakis, Nicholas A., and James H. Fowler. 2011. *Connected: The
Surprising Power of Our Social Networks and How They Shape Our
Lives*. New York: Back Bay Books.

Covey, Stephen M. R., and Rebecca R. Merrill. 2018. *The Speed of Trust:
The One Thing That Changes Everything*. New York: Free Press.

DeHayes, Jennifer. 2019. "The Power of Trust." Filmed October 29, 2019,
in Farmingdale, NY. TED video, 17:08.
https://www.ted.com/talks/jennifer_dehayes_the_power_of_trust.

FranklinCovey. n.d. "Stephen M. R. Covey." Accessed August 20, 2022.
https://www.franklincovey.com/speakers-bureau/stephen-m-
covey/.

Gartner. 2021. "Gartner HR Research Reveals 82% of Employees Report
Working Environment Lacks Fairness."
https://www.gartner.com/en/newsroom/press-releases/2021-08-
11-gartner-hr-research-reveals-eighty-two-percent-of-employees-
report-working-environment-lacks-fairness (accessed October 15,
2022).

Greenleaf, Robert K., Larry C. Spears, Stephen R. Covey, and Peter
M. Senge. 2002. *Servant Leadership: A Journey into the Nature of
Legitimate Power and Greatness*. New York: Paulist Press.

Hayasaki, Erika. 2018. "Identical Twins Hint at How Environments Change Gene Expression." The Atlantic. https://www.theatlantic.com/science/archive/2018/05/twin-epigenetics/560189/ (accessed October 15, 2022).

Heal the Divide Podinar. 2020. "The Empathy Effect: 7 Keys to Transformation with Dr. Helen Riess" YouTube. August 27, 2020. Educational video, 53:07. https://www.youtube.com/watch?v=W2074HHAQwQ.

Insights for Entrepreneurs. 2018. "How to Lead Introverts" YouTube. January 29, 2018. Educational video, 1:40. https://www.youtube.com/watch?v=bbhctpQVyJk.

Ladika, Susan. 2021. "The Value of Trust." SHRM. https://www.shrm.org/hr-today/news/hr-magazine/summer2021/pages/the-value-of-trust.aspx (accessed October 15, 2022).

Leading Effectively Staff. 2020. "The Importance of Empathy in the Workplace." Center for Creative Leadership. https://www.ccl.org/articles/leading-effectively-articles/empathy-in-the-workplace-a-tool-for-effective-leadership (accessed October 15, 2022).

Lockheed Martin. n.d. "The F-35B: First Descent." Accessed August 20, 2022. https://www.lockheedmartin.com/en-us/news/features/history/f35b.html.

Marine Mammal Science Podcast. "MMS 88: Altruism in Whales." May 22, 2021. Podcast, MP3 audio, 29:27. https://sites.libsyn.com/203687/mms-88-altruism-in-whales.

Marsh, Abigail. 2016. "Why Some People Are More Altruistic than Others." Filmed September 16, 2016, in Banff, Alberta. TED video, 12:13. https://www.ted.com/talks/abigail_marsh_why_some_people_are_more_altruistic_than_others.

Nutt, Amy Ellis. 2021. "Why Fear Motivates Both Altruists and Psychopaths." The Washington Post. https://www.washingtonpost.com/news/speaking-of-science/wp/2017/11/21/why-fear-motivates-both-altruists-and-psychopaths/ (accessed October 15, 2022).

Prime, Jeanine, and Elizabeth Salib. 2014. "The Best Leaders Are Humble Leaders." Harvard Business Review. https://hbr.org/2014/05/the-best-leaders-are-humble-leaders (accessed October 15, 2022).

Riess, Helen, and Liz Neporent. 2018. *The Empathy Effect: Seven Neuroscience-Based Keys for Transforming the Way We Live, Love, Work, and Connect across Differences.* Boulder, CO: Sounds True.

Rovelli, Carlo. 2017. *Reality Is Not What It Seems: The Journey to Quantum Gravity.* New York: Riverhead Books. Kindle.

Sahu, Monalisha, and Josyula G. Prasuna. 2016. "Twin Studies: A Unique Epidemiological Tool." *Indian Journal of Community Medicine* 41, 177-82. https://doi.org/10.4103/0970-0218.183593.

Seifert, Matthias, Joel Brockner, Emily C. Bianchi, and Henry Moon. 2015. "How Workplace Fairness Affects Employee Commitment." MIT Sloan Management Review. https://sloanreview.mit.edu/article/how-workplace-fairness-affects-employee-commitment (accessed October 15, 2022).

Shahar, Noga. 2021. "New Research Exposes the Biological Basis of Empathy." Neuroscience News. https://neurosciencenews.com/reward-system-empathy-19381/ (accessed October 15, 2022).

Spector, Candace. 2021. "Sho-Ban Tribes Honor First Woman to Fly F-35B Jets in Marine Corps." Idaho State Journal. https://www.postregister.com/chronicle/freeaccess/sho-ban-tribes-honor-first-woman-to-fly-f-35b-jets-in-marine-corps/article_3530795e-05ce-596a-b895-ee1b81519bb1.html (accessed October 15, 2022).

Van Bommel, Tara. 2021. "The Power of Empathy in Times of Crisis and Beyond." Catalyst. https://www.catalyst.org/reports/empathy-work-strategy-crisis.

Vella, Brittney. 2019. "First Female F-35B Pilot." United States Marine Corps. https://www.marines.mil/News/News-Display/Article/1930080/first-female-f-35b-pilot (accessed October 15, 2022).

Wein, Harrison. 2015. "Rats Show Empathy, Too." National Institutes of Health. U.S. Department of Health and Human Services. https://www.nih.gov/news-events/nih-research-matters/rats-show-empathy-too (accessed October 15, 2022).

Zak, Paul J. 2017. "The Neuroscience of Trust." Harvard Business Review.
https://hbr.org/2017/01/the-neuroscience-of-trust (accessed October 15, 2022).

LEAD YOUR TEAM

Al, Stefan. 2020. "The Air-Conditioned Cowboy: A History of El Rancho Vegas." The MIT Press Reader.
https://thereader.mitpress.mit.edu/the-air-conditioned-cowboy-el-rancho (accessed October 15, 2022).

Duarte. N.d. "Meet Nancy." Accessed August 22, 2022.
https://www.duarte.com/nancy-duarte/.

Duarte, Nancy, and Patti Sanchez. 2016. *Illuminate: Ignite Change through Speeches, Stories, Ceremonies, and Symbols.* New York: Portfolio/Penguin.

Edmondson, Amy C. 2004. "Learning from Mistakes Is Easier Said than Done." *The Journal of Applied Behavioral Science* 40, no. 1: 66–90.
https://doi.org/10.1177/0021886304263849.

Edmondson, Amy C. 2019. *The Fearless Organization: Creating Psychological Safety in the Workplace for Learning, Innovation, and Growth.* Hoboken, NJ: Wiley.

Ellemers, Naomi, Ed Sleebos, Daan Stam, and Dick de Gilder. 2011. "Feeling Included and Valued: How Perceived Respect Affects Positive Team Identity and Willingness to Invest in the Team." *British Journal of Management* 24, no. 1: 21–37. https://doi.org/10.1111/j.1467-8551.2011.00784.x.

Ennis, Robert H. 1993. "Critical Thinking Assessment." *Theory Into Practice* 32, no. 3 (Summer): 179–86. http://www.jstor.org/stable/1476699.

Evans, Cindy, and Will Stefanov. 2008. "Cities at Night: The View from Space." NASA. https://earthobservatory.nasa.gov/features/CitiesAtNight (accessed October 15, 2022).

Grant, Adam. "Is It Safe to Speak up at Work?" WorkLife with Adam Grant, July 19, 2021. Podcast, MP3 audio, 37:19. https://podcasts.apple.com/us/podcast/is-it-safe-to-speak-up-at-work/id1346314086?i=1000529425087.

Gratton, Lynda, and Tamara J. Erickson. 2007. "Eight Ways to Build Collaborative Teams." Harvard Business Review. https://hbr.org/2007/11/eight-ways-to-build-collaborative-teams (accessed October 15, 2022).

Griffiths, Sarah. 2016. "Baddies in Movies Help to Set Our Moral Compass and Help Us Spot Evil in Real Life." Daily Mail Online, https://www.dailymail.co.uk/sciencetech/article-3404773/Super-villains-force-GOOD-Baddies-movies-help-set-moral-compass-help-spot-evil-real-life.html (accessed October 15, 2022).

Haas, Martine, and Mark Mortensen. 2016. "The Secrets of Great Teamwork." Harvard Business Review https://hbr.org/2016/06/the-secrets-of-great-teamwork (accessed October 15, 2022).

Han, GuoHong (Helen) and Harms, Peter D., 2010. "Team identification, trust, and conflict: A mediation model". *International Journal of Conflict Management* 21, no. 1: 20-43. https://doi.org/10.1108/10444061011016614.

Hitchcock, David. 2018. "Critical Thinking." Stanford Encyclopedia of Philosophy. https://plato.stanford.edu/entries/critical-thinking (accessed October 15, 2022).

Hopkins, A. D. 1999. "Thomas Hull." Las Vegas Review-Journal.. https://www.reviewjournal.com/news/thomas-hull (accessed October 15, 2022).

Horridge, Kevin. 2017. "8 Men Who Helped Build Vegas." Casino.org https://www.casino.org/blog/8-men-who-built-vegas (accessed October 15, 2022).

Jha, Sumi. 2019. "Team Psychological Safety and Team Performance." *International Journal of Organizational Analysis* 27, no. 4: 903–24. https://doi.org/10.1108/ijoa-10-2018-1567.

Judson, Gillian. 2021. "Cultivating Leadership Imagination with Cognitive Tools: An Imagination-Focused Approach to Leadership Education." *Journal of Research on Leadership Education*, 0, no. 0. https://doi.org/10.1177/19427751211022028.

Li, Li-Li, Joshua M. Plotnik, Shang-Wen Xia, Estelle Meaux, and Rui-Chang Quan. 2021. "Cooperating Elephants Mitigate Competition until the Stakes Get Too High." *PLOS Biology* 19, no. 9: 1-23. https://doi.org/10.1371/journal.pbio.3001391.

Lucas, George, director. 1977. *Star Wars Episode IV: A New Hope.* Twentieth Century Fox 2 hr., 1 min.

Mahembe, Bright, and Amos S. Engelbrecht. 2013. "The Relationship between Servant Leadership, Affective Team Commitment and Team Effectiveness." *SA Journal of Human Resource Management* 11, no. 1: 1-10. https://doi.org/10.4102/sajhrm.v11i1.495.

Maximo, Natasha, Marius W. Stander, and Lynelle Coxen. 2019. "Authentic Leadership and Work Engagement: The Indirect Effects of Psychological Safety and Trust in Supervisors." *SA Journal of Industrial Psychology* 45: 1-11. https://doi.org/10.4102/sajip.v45i0.1612.

Moorehead, Liz. "59 Best Sales Team Names That Are Clever, Funny, and Only for Closers." IMPACT Inbound Marketing Agency. https://www.impactplus.com/blog/sales-team-names (accessed October 15, 2022).

Mudrack, Peter E. 1989. "Defining Group Cohesiveness." *Small Group Behavior* 20, no. 1 (February): 37–49. https://doi.org/10.1177/104649648902000103.

"Nets @ 76ers." n.d. National Basketball Association. Accessed August 22, 2022. https://www.nba.com/game/njn-vs-phl-0027800130/box-score (accessed October 15, 2022).

Plummer, Matt. 2021. "A Short Guide to Building Your Team's Critical Thinking Skills." Harvard Business Review. https://hbr.org/2019/10/a-short-guide-to-building-your-teams-critical-thinking-skills (accessed October 15, 2022).

Powell, Shaun. 2018. "In 1978-79 Season, Deal like No Other Happened at NBA Trade Deadline." National Basketball Association, February 6. https://www.nba.com/news/philadelphia-76ers-new-jersey-nets-crazy-game-trade-1978-79-season (accessed October 15, 2022).

Reis, Daniela Pinheiro, and Katia Puente-Palacios. 2019. "Team Effectiveness: The Predictive Role of Team Identity." *RAUSP Management Journal* 54, no. 2: 141–53. https://doi.org/10.1108/rausp-07-2018-0046.

Schwantes, Marcel. "Do You Foster Psychological Safety?" Love in Action Podcast, March 16, 2022. Podcast, MP3 audio, 5:48. https://podcasts.apple.com/us/podcast/do-you-foster-psychological-safety/id1456073489?i=1000554326508.

"Scrum Team Names: 150+ Best Agile Team Names!" Remote Tools. Accessed. https://www.remote.tools/remote-work/scrum-team-names (accessed October 15, 2022).

Sheng, Chieh-Wen, Yi-Fang Tian, and Ming-Chia Chen. "Relationships among Teamwork Behavior, Trust, Perceived Team Support,
and Team Commitment." *Scientific Journal Publishers*, (1970).
https://doi.org/10.2224/sbp.2010.38.10.1297.

Society for Human Resource Management (SHRM). 2019. "2019 State
of the Workplace: Exploring the Impact of the Skills Gap and
Employment-Based Immigration." Accessed October 15, 2022.
https://www.shrm.org/about-shrm/Documents/SHRM%20
State%20of%20Workplace_Bridging%20the%20Talent%20Gap.pdf.

Summers, Irvin, Terry Coffelt, and Roy E. Horton. 1988. "Work-Group
Cohesion." *Psychological Reports* 63, no. 2 (October): 627–36.
https://doi.org/10.2466/pr0.1988.63.2.627.

Zeiger, Mimi. 2016. "From Nets to Networks." Architect Magazine.
https://www.architectmagazine.com/technology/lighting/from-
nets-to-networks_o (accessed October 15, 2022).

LEAD YOUR ORGANIZATION

Ahmad, Shoeb. 2020. "The Corporate Culture and Employees' Performance: An Overview." *Journal of Management and Science* 10, no.
3: 1–6.
https://doi.org/10.26524/jms.10.1.

Alagaraja, Meera, and Brad Shuck. 2015. "Exploring Organizational
Alignment-Employee Engagement Linkages and Impact on Individual Performance." *Human Resource Development Review* 14, no.
1 (March): 17–37.
https://doi.org/10.1177/1534484314549455.

Bartkus, Barbara R., and Myron Glassman. 2008. "Do Firms Practice What They Preach? The Relationship between Mission Statements and Stakeholder Management." *Journal of Business Ethics* 83, no. 2 (December): 207–16. http://www.jstor.org/stable/25482367.

Beaver Solutions. n.d. "Beaver Benefits — A Keystone Species." Accessed September 1, 2022. https://www.beaversolutions.com/beaver-facts-education/beaver-benefits-a-keystone-species/.

Berson, Yair, Shaul Oreg, and Taly Dvir. 2008. "CEO Values, Organizational Culture and Firm Outcomes." *Journal of Organizational Behavior* 29, no. 5 (July): 615–33. http://www.jstor.org/stable/30162650.

B Lab. n.d. "B Corp Certification Demonstrates a Company's Entire Social and Environmental Impact." Accessed September 1, 2022. https://www.bcorporation.net/en-us/certification.

Brain, Marshall, Charles W. Bryant, and Clint Pumphrey. 2021. "How Batteries Work." HowStuffWorks. https://electronics.howstuffworks.com/everyday-tech/battery5.htm (accessed October 15, 2022).

Byles, Charles M., Kenneth E. Aupperle, and Bernard Arogyaswamy. 1991. "Organizational Culture And Performance." *Journal of Managerial Issues* 3, no. 4 (Winter): 512–27. http://www.jstor.org/stable/40603778.

Cardona, Pablo, and Carlos Rey. 2022. "Is There a Link between Corporate Purpose and Performance?" *Management by Missions* (January): 3–19. https://doi.org/10.1007/978-3-030-83780-8_1.

Carrick, Evie. 2021. "The World's Fastest High-Speed Trains." Travel + Leisure. https://www.travelandleisure.com/trip-ideas/bus-train/fastest-trains-in-the-world (accessed October 15, 2022).

Cortés-Sánchez, Julián David, and Liliana Rivera. 2019. "Mission Statements and Financial Performance in Latin-American Firms." *Business: Theory and Practice* 20: 270–83. https://doi.org/10.3846/btp.2019.26.

"Creating a Culture like Netflix's with Patty McCord." The EntreLeadership Podcast, February 12, 2018. Podcast, MP3 audio, 45:49. https://podcasts.apple.com/us/podcast/the-entreleadership-podcast/id435836905?i=1000402039590.

Diez-Busto, Elsa, Lidia Sanchez-Ruiz, and Ana Fernandez-Laviada. 2021. "The B Corp Movement: A Systematic Literature Review." *Sustainability* 13, no. 5: 2508. https://doi.org/10.3390/su13052508.

Doerr, John E. 2018. *Measure What Matters: How Google, Bono, and the Gates Foundation Rock the World with OKRs.* New York: Portfolio/Penguin.

Glazer, Robert. "Julie Ann Sullivan on Building a Culture Employees Love." Elevate with Robert Glazer, October 6, 2020. Podcast, MP3 audio, 36:02.
https://podcasts.apple.com/us/podcast/julie-ann-sullivan-on-building-a-culture-employees-love/id1454045560?i=1000493772039.

Gong.io. "How to Harness the Power of Your Mission Statement on Apple Podcasts." Reveal: The Revenue Intelligence Podcast, April 11, 2021. Podcast, MP3 audio, 45:59.
https://podcasts.apple.com/sv/podcast/how-to-harness-the-power-of-your-mission-statement/id1486617071?i=1000516741079.

Hamar, Brent, Carter Coberley, James E. Pope, and Elizabeth Y. Rula. 2015. "Well-Being Improvement in a Midsize Employer: Changes in Well-Being, Productivity, Health Risk, and Perceived Employer Support After Implementation of a Well-Being Improvement Strategy." *Journal of Occupational and Environmental Medicine* 57, no. 4 (April): 367–73.
https://www.jstor.org/stable/48500738.

Hooper, M. J., and T. Pye. 2002. "Company Culture: The Relationship of Organizational Values to Business Excellence." *Journal of Human Values* 8, no. 1 (June): 27–43.
https://doi.org/10.1177/097168580200800104.

Joly, Hubert. 2021. *The Heart of Business: Leadership Principles for the Next Era of Capitalism.* Boston, MA: Harvard Business Review Press.

Kaplan, Robert S., and David P. Norton. 2006. *Alignment: Using the Balanced Scorecard to Create Corporate Synergies.* Boston, MA: Harvard Business School Press.

Kavanaugh, Jeff, and Rafee Tarafdar. 2021. *The Live Enterprise: Create a Continuously Evolving and Learning Organization*. New York: McGraw Hill.

Liu, David. 2022. "Laura Putnam of Motion Infusion on 5 Ways That Businesses Can Help Promote the Mental Wellness of..." Authority Magazine. https://medium.com/authority-magazine/laura-putnam-of-motion-infusion-on-5-ways-that-businesses-can-help-promote-the-mental-wellness-of-29aa682283ef (accessed October 15, 2022).

Mackey, John, and Rajendra Sisodia. 2014. *Conscious Capitalism: Liberating the Heroic Spirit of Business*. Boston, MA: Harvard Business Review Press.

Mattke, Soeren, Hangsheng Liu, John P. Caloyeras, Christina Y. Huang, Kristin R. Van Busum, Dmitry Khodyakov, and Victoria Shier. 2013. "Lessons from Case Studies for Program Implementation." In *Workplace Wellness Programs Study: Final Report* (Rand Corporation, 2013): 93–104. http://www.jstor.org/stable/10.7249/j.ctt3fgzhg.12.

McCord, Patty. 2017. *Powerful: Building a Culture of Freedom and Responsibility: From the Co-Creator of Netflix Culture Deck*. San Francisco, CA: Silicon Guild.

Murray, Alan, and Catherine Whitney. 2022. *Tomorrow's Capitalist: My Search for the Soul of Business*. New York: PublicAffairs, Hachette Book Group.

National Geographic Society. n.d. "Role of Keystone Species in an Ecosystem." Accessed September 1, 2022. https://education.nationalgeographic.org/resource/role-keystone-species-ecosystem.

Oswald, Andrew J., Eugenio Proto, and Daniel Sgroi. 2015. "Happiness and Productivity." *Journal of Labor Economics* 33, no. 4 (October): 789–822. https://doi.org/10.1086/681096.

Paine, Lynn Sharp. 2003. *Value Shift: Why Companies Must Merge Social and Financial Imperatives to Achieve Superior Performance.* London: McGraw Hill.

Ramsey Network. "Creating a Culture like Netflix's with Patty McCord." The EntreLeadership Podcast, February 12, 2018. https://podcasts.apple.com/us/podcast/the-entreleadership-podcast/id435836905?i=1000402039590.

Sinek, Simon. 2009. *Start with Why: How Great Leaders Inspire Everyone to Take Action.* London: Portfolio/Penguin.

Taylor, Anthony. "How to Create a Continuously Learning & Evolving Organization - w/ Jeff Kavanaugh Ep#91." SME Strategy: Strategy & Leadership Podcast, February 24, 2021. Podcast, MP3 audio, 41:54. https://www.smestrategy.net/blog/create-a-continuously-learning-evolving-organization.

Trevor, Jonathan. 2018. "Is Anyone in Your Company Paying Attention to Strategic Alignment?" Harvard Business Review. https://hbr.org/2018/01/is-anyone-in-your-company-paying-attention-to-strategic-alignment (accessed October 15, 2022).

Winston, Andrew. 2021. "Is the Business Roundtable Statement Just
   Empty Rhetoric?" Harvard Business Review.
   https://hbr.org/2019/08/is-the-business-roundtable-statement-
   just-empty-rhetoric (accessed October 15, 2022).

Wright, Thomas A., and Ching-Chu Huang. 2012. "The Many Benefits
   of Employee Well-Being in Organizational Research." *Journal of
   Organizational Behavior* 33, no. 8 (November): 1188–92.
   https://doi.org/10.1002/job.1828.

LEAD THE WORLD

Acumen. n.d. "Jacqueline Novogratz, Founder and CEO of Acumen."
   Accessed September 4, 2022.
   https://acumen.org/jacqueline-novogratz/.

Bonini, Sheila. 2021. "The Coca-Cola and WWF Partnership: Working
   Toward a Resilient Future." World Wildlife Fund.
   https://www.worldwildlife.org/blogs/sustainability-works/posts/
   the-coca-cola-and-wwf-partnership-working-toward-a-resilient-
   future (accessed October 15, 2022).

Brennan, Dan, ed. 2021. "Work and Family Balance: How It Affects
   Your Mental Health." WebMD.
   https://www.webmd.com/balance/balancing-work-and-family
   (accessed October 15, 2022).

The Coca-Cola Company. n.d. "2020 World without Waste Report."
   Accessed September 4, 2022.
   https://www.coca-colacompany.com/reports/world-without-
   waste-2020.

The Coca-Cola Company, n.d. "About." Accessed September 4, 2022.
https://investors.coca-colacompany.com/about.

The Coca-Cola Company. n.d. "What Is World without Waste?"
Accessed September 4, 2022.
https://www.coca-colacompany.com/faqs/what-is-world-without-waste.

Cole Haan Brandvoice. "Changemakers: Changing the World, One Silicone
Bag at a Time." Forbes Magazine.
https://www.forbes.com/sites/colehaan/2020/01/28/changemakers-chang-
ing-the-world-one-silicone-bag-at-a-time/ (accessed October 15, 2022).

Colosi, Rosie. 2019. "This Military Spouse Couldn't Find Anyone to Hire
Her-so She Created a Company That Would." MSNBC.
https://www.msnbc.com/know-your-value/military-spouse-could-
n-t-find-anyone-hire-her-so-she-n1079366 (accessed October 15,
2022).

Danley, Lucy. 2021. "New Pew Study Highlights Child Care Struggles
for Working Parents." First Five Years Fund.
https://www.ffyf.org/new-pew-study-highlights-child-care-strug-
gles-for-working-parents/ (accessed October 15, 2022).

DiversityInc. 2019. "Hilton Expands Family-Friendly Benefits, Extends
Parental Leave."
https://www.diversityinc.com/hilton-expands-family-friend-
ly-benefits-extends-parental-leave/ (accessed October 15, 2022).

Francome, Will, Megan Garner, and Elliot Stein. 2020. "Welcome to
Monowi, Nebraska: Population 1." BBC Travel.
https://www.bbc.com/travel/article/20180129-welcome-to-monow-
i-nebraska-population-1 (accessed October 15, 2022).

Global Citizen. 2017. "Coca-Cola Produced More than 110 Billion Plastic Bottles Last Year." EcoWatch. https://www.ecowatch.com/coca-cola-plastic-bottles-2492093659.html (accessed October 15, 2022).

Gordon, Jonathan, and Nola Taylor Tilman. 2022. "How Big Is the Universe?" https://www.space.com/24073-how-big-is-the-universe.html (accessed October 15, 2022).

Greyson, Bruce. 2021. *After: A Doctor Explores What Near-Death Experiences Reveal about Life and Beyond*. New York, NY: St. Martin's Essentials, an imprint of St. Martin's Publishing Group.

Guinness World Records. n.d. "Largest Recycled Plastic Sculpture (Supported)." Accessed September 4, 2022. https://www.guinnessworldrecords.com/world-records/542843-largest-recycled-plastic-sculpture-supported.

Habitat for Humanity. n.d. "About Habitat for Humanity." Accessed September 4, 2022. https://www.habitat.org/about.

Habitat for Humanity. n.d. "Corporate Giving." Accessed September 4, 2022. https://www.habitat.org/support/corporate-giving.

Habitat for Humanity. n.d. "Corporate and Foundation Partners." Accessed September 4, 2022. https://www.habitat.org/about/partners/corporate-and-foundation.

Habitat for Humanity. n.d. "Habitat Advocate and Volunteer Shares Her Personal Journey." https://www.habitat.org/stories/habitat-advocate-and-volunteer-shares-her-personal-journey.

Hiring Our Heroes. n.d. "Shaping the Future of Military Spouse Employment by Advocating for Legislative Action." U.S. Chamber of Commerce Foundation. https://www.hiringourheroes.org/2021-military-spouse-employment-summit-highlights/

Jones, Roger. 2016. "The Family Dynamics We Grew up with Shape How We Work." Harvard Business Review. https://hbr.org/2016/07/the-family-dynamics-we-grew-up-with-shape-how-we-work

Knapp, Fred. 2021. "Community Celebrates Elsie Eiler, Monowi Tavern." Nebraska Public Media. https://nebraskapublicmedia.org/en/news/news-articles/neighbors-celebrate-elsie-eiler-monowi-tavern/ (accessed October 15, 2022).

Lencioni, Patrick. 2008. *The 3 Big Questions for a Frantic Family: A Leadership Fable- about Restoring Sanity to the Most Important Organization in Your Life.* San Francisco, CA: Jossey-Bass.

Lifewater International. 2020. "9 World Poverty Statistics That Everyone Should Know." https://lifewater.org/blog/9-world-poverty-statistics-to-know-today/ (accessed October 15, 2022).

Mortensen, Christine. 2020. "SPRK'd Founders Spotlight: Michelle Penczak, CEO of Squared Away." LinkedIn. https://www.linkedin.com/pulse/sprkd-founders-spotlight-michelle-penczak-ceo-squared-mortensen/ (accessed October 15, 2022).

Murphy, Kevin. 2011. "Nebraska Woman Is Mayor and Only Resident, of Rural Town." https://www.reuters.com/article/us-census-town/nebraska-woman-is-mayor-and-only-resident-of-rural-town-idUS-TRE7311Y620110402 (accessed October 15, 2022).

NobelPrize.org. n.d. "The Nobel Prize Organisation." https://www.nobelprize.org/the-nobel-prize-organisation/.

Novogratz, Jacqueline. 2010. *The Blue Sweater: Bridging the Gap between Rich and Poor in an Interconnected World.* New York: Rodale.

Novogratz, Jacqueline. "Inspiring a Life of Immersion." Filmed December 2010 in Washington, DC. TED video, 17:30. https://www.ted.com/talks/jacqueline_novogratz_inspiring_a_life_of_immersion.

Opel, Kelsey. 2021. "38% Military Spouse Unemployment Rate: How We're Changing This." Medium. https://medium.com/squaredaway/38-military-spouse-unemployment-rate-how-were-changing-this-9cd85258294 (accessed October 15, 2022).

Polman, Paul, and C. B. Bhattacharya. 2016. "Engaging Employees to Create a Sustainable Business." *Stanford Social Innovation Review* 14, no. 4 (Fall): 34-39. https://ssir.org/articles/entry/engaging_employees_to_create_a_sustainable_business.

Raz, Guy, Kerry Thompson, and Neva Grant. 2021. "Stasher and Modern Twist: Kat Nouri." NPR, November 22. https://www.npr.org/2021/11/19/1057386872/stasher-and-modern-twist-kat-nouri (accessed October 15, 2022).

Recycle Coach. 2020. "6 Examples of Sustainability in the Workplace (and Their Impact)." https://recyclecoach.com/blog/6-examples-of-sustainability-in-the-workplace-and-their-impact/ (accessed October 15, 2022).

Socio, Mike De. 2021. "Coke and Pepsi Eye New Sustainability Goals after Years of Failed Promises." Fortune. https://fortune.com/2021/06/22/coke-pepsi-sustainability-goals/ (accessed October 15, 2022).

Spectrum Integrators. 2022. "Are Near-Death Experiences Real?" YouTube. September 17, 2022. Educational video, 1:06:25. https://www.youtube.com/watch?v=Bg7W9mODkC4.

Stories from Hilton. 2019. "Hilton Named #1 Best Workplace for Parents." https://stories.hilton.com/releases/hilton-named-1-best-workplace-for-parents-for-second-year-in-a-row (accessed October 15, 2022).

Tägil, Sven. 1998. "Alfred Nobel's Thoughts about War and Peace." NobelPrize.org. https://www.nobelprize.org/alfred-nobel/alfred-nobels-thoughts-about-war-and-peace/ (accessed October 15, 2022).

"Tips for Families: Everyday Leadership Skills." U.S. Department of Health and Human Services. https://eclkc.ohs.acf.hhs.gov/publication/tips-families-every-day-leadership-skills (accessed October 15, 2022).

UNICEF. n.d. "10 Ways Companies Can Be More Family-Friendly." https://www.unicef.org/early-childhood-develop-ment/10-ways-companies-can-be-more-family-friendly.

Wright, Tom. 2018. "Artists Build Life-Size Blue Whale out of Plastic Trash for Monterey Bay Aquarium." Monterey Herald. https://www.montereyherald.com/2018/10/11/artists-build-life-size-blue-whale-out-of-plastic-trash-for-monterey-bay-aquarium/ (accessed October 15, 2022).

Year Up. n.d. "About." Accessed September 4, 2022. https://www.yearup.org/about.

ACTION—STEPS ALONG THE PATH

Christakis, Nicholas A., and James H. Fowler. 2011. *Connected: The Surprising Power of Our Social Networks and How They Shape Our Lives*. New York: Back Bay Books.

Covey, Stephen M. R., and Rebecca R. Merrill. 2018. *The Speed of Trust: The One Thing That Changes Everything*. New York: Free Press.

Duarte, Nancy, and Patti Sanchez. 2016. *Illuminate: Ignite Change through Speeches, Stories, Ceremonies, and Symbols.* New York: Portfolio/Penguin.

Edmondson, Amy C. 2019. *The Fearless Organization: Creating Psychological Safety in the Workplace for Learning, Innovation, and Growth.* Hoboken, NJ: Wiley.

Eurich, Tasha. 2017. *Insight: Why We're Not as Self-Aware as We Think, and How Seeing Ourselves Clearly Helps Us Succeed at Work and in Life.* New York: Crown Business.

McCord, Patty. 2017. *Powerful: Building a Culture of Freedom and Responsibility: From the Co-Creator of Netflix Culture Deck.* San Francisco: Silicon Guild.

Novogratz, Jacqueline. 2010. *The Blue Sweater: Bridging the Gap between Rich and Poor in an Interconnected World.* New York: Rodale.

Paine, Lynn Sharp. 2003. *Value Shift: Why Companies Must Merge Social and Financial Imperatives to Achieve Superior Performance.* London: McGraw Hill.

Putnam, Laura. 2015. *Workplace Wellness That Works: 10 Steps to Infuse Well-Being and Vitality into Any Organization.* Hoboken, NJ: John Wiley & Sons.

Sinek, Simon. 2009. *Start with Why: How Great Leaders Inspire Everyone to Take Action.* New York: Portfolio/Penguin.

TIPS FOR EXECUTIVES

Kruse, Kevin. 2022. "From the CEO Down, and from the Frontline up: How ZoomInfo Develops Great Leaders." Forbes, May 10. https://www.forbes.com/sites/kevinkruse/2022/05/06/from-the-ceo-down-and-from-the-frontline-up-how-zoominfo-develops-great-leaders/?sh=303ec6ba2b20 (accessed October 15, 2022).

Nasdaq. n.d. "ZI Financials." https://www.nasdaq.com/market-activity/stocks/zi/financials.

Sheridan, Richard. 2018. *Chief Joy Officer: How Great Leaders Elevate Human Energy and Eliminate Fear.* New York: Portfolio/Penguin, An Imprint of Penguin Random House LLC.

Wiles, Jackie. 2022. "CEOs Turn a Sharp Eye to Workforce Issues and Sustainability in 2022-23." Gartner https://www.gartner.com/en/articles/ceos-turn-a-sharp-eye-to-work-force-issues-and-sustainability-in-2022-23 (accessed October 15, 2022).

TIPS FOR HR LEADERS

Aldrich, Berta. 2021. *Winning the Talent Shift: Three Steps to Unleashing the New High Performance Workplace.* Hoboken, NJ: John Wiley & Sons, Inc.

Made in the USA
Middletown, DE
29 April 2024